Leading Christian Communities

Leading Christian Communities

C. Kavin Rowe

William B. Eerdmans Publishing Company
Grand Rapids, Michigan

Wm. B. Eerdmans Publishing Co.
4035 Park East Court SE, Grand Rapids, Michigan 49546
www.eerdmans.com

Published 2023
Printed in the United States of America

29 28 27 26 25 24 23   1 2 3 4 5 6 7

ISBN 978-0-8028-8272-1

Library of Congress Cataloging-in-Publication Data

A catalog record for this book is available from the Library of Congress.

The essays included here were first published in *Faith & Leadership*,
www.faithandleadership.com, and are reprinted here by permission.

Contents

CONTENTS

Preface

The overall goal of these brief essays is to display the shape and dynamics of Christian thinking when it is biblically shaped and focused on critical questions Christian leaders face. Some of the essays directly engage topics crucial to effective leadership (e.g., humor), some draw out the implications of the connections between various Christian affirmations (e.g., Christmas and Easter), and some develop generative ways of thinking about fundamental rhythms that are inherent to fruitful Christian life (e.g., traditioned innovation). What ties them together is not a single theme or a particular methodology but the conviction that Christian life is an integrated whole. God made and is redeeming all that is. Christians ought, therefore, to be interested in everything, and we should seek to relate all things to God. Indeed, this is a—maybe *the*—central task in Christian leadership and stewarding institutions. We should not think as if God does not matter for what we think about, as if reflecting on "success" or "hierarchy" or "community" could be done in abstraction from the way in which such matters get their meaning inside a Christian understanding of reality. Could we think without reference to God, we would not need specifically Christian consideration of leadership questions; we could simply read the *Harvard Business Review* or other well-tailored publications for general audiences and learn what we needed to know. But coming to an understanding of how Christians can address such questions requires thinking through the most basic difference between an already-available understanding and one that is rooted in God's self-disclosure in Christ and the Scripture that witnesses to Christ. If these essays are helpful, it will be because they depend on that kind of thinking for the sense they make.

Thanks are due to James Ernest of Eerdmans for his long-time kindness and his eagerness to publish these essays. Thanks to James's vision, this is volume 1 of a three-volume collection of my essays. Thanks are also due to Dr. Brad Boswell, who did the labor needed to prepare the manuscript, and to Aaron Ebert, who proofread and made the index.

Part 1

The Acts of the Apostles and Thriving Communities

The Pattern of Life
in Thriving Communities

Our work as Christian leaders is to cultivate thriving communities that are foretastes of the kingdom of God. The Acts of the Apostles pressures us to see six features that are the essence of the church.

What makes a community thrive?

As Christian leaders, we tend to assume we already know what thriving communities are; we then simply go looking for instances in Scripture that confirm our knowledge and agenda. Over time, we cease learning from Scripture how to think and instead use it as a tool to back up our cherished beliefs.

But the scriptural texts are not inert matter, words on the page simply waiting for verbal activation, or "ideas" asking for our intellectual assent. Scripture, so Christians confess, has the ability to effect change in the reader for the sake of the kingdom of God, to exert directive pressure upon our thinking by means of a fundamental transformation of life.

Indeed, the possibility for transformation is finally why we continue to return to the Bible: again and again, we sense that our resources, taken alone, are not enough for the magnitude of the task, that we need more than a new set of tools or a different theory under which to conceptualize our work. What we need in order to create and nurture communities that thrive as foretastes of the kingdom of God is a deep and abiding direction. Inasmuch as it actively orders and reorders our thought—continually tutors us in how to think—Scripture's pressure is this deep and abiding direction from God.

The Acts of the Apostles is a particularly rich scriptural source for the kinds of questions we need to ask. Acts is the only biblical text that narrates the formation of early Christian communities in their earliest days. It corresponds, therefore, to the theological shape of God's work in establishing communities that were meant to thrive. Acts offers us six features of a pattern of life in thriving communities— not a "to-do" list, but a picture of what the church needs to continue being the church. To put it like this is to emphasize the fact that we cannot pick or choose which of the six features we like: according to the narrative of Acts, all six have to be there for the church to be the church (which is but another way of saying that the narrative of Acts is close to unimaginable without all six features).

1. Networks and networking

Some Christians do not like the thought of networking. To them it feels disingenuous, and they worry, often rightly, about a kind of schmoozing that is in bad taste. But socially embarrassing or morally questionable schmoozing is hardly what we see in Acts, and there is no better name for the activity of the early Christians in establishing relationships between the churches than *networking*.

Networking as a feature of early Christian existence emerges most clearly in the mission to the gentiles. If one reads Acts while consulting a detailed map of the Mediterranean world in the first century, it is easy to see that the predominant strategy of the first Christians was to build their communities in major urban centers where the resources were plentiful: personnel, main roads, letter carriers, boats, travelers, trade, and so on. Caesarea, Tyre, Sidon, Ephesus, Corinth, Philippi, Thessalonica—these and many others were all ports or cities that lay along major roads in the Roman Empire. The early Christians used the advantages of such places to develop communities that could have easy contact with one another and could become, by means of their

4

communication and interconnection, "brothers and sisters" in Christ. The distinctive Christian familial language, that is, has the social reality of networking as its presupposition.

Reading Acts carefully will disclose a remarkable level of interconnection between the various Christian communities in terms of both personnel and communication by letter and/or messenger. The Jerusalem council assumes its letter will reach the Christian communities scattered around the rim of the Mediterranean. And tracing Paul's travel through his various journeys is an exercise in visiting and revisiting churches in virtually all parts east of Rome. In this way, the narrative of Acts helps to make concrete and intelligible the numerous greetings and personal instructions we see, for example, in Paul's letters. According to Acts, the early Christians were fully networked.

2. Visibility

One of the most powerful and, in a sense, most pernicious dichotomies in the modern West is the public-private split. The effect of this dichotomy has been to privatize religion. One's religion is not, for example, supposed to interfere in politics or play a part in a secular university classroom or a public school. Christianity is what one does or says in a "personal" sphere, in private.

The Acts of the Apostles knows nothing of this dichotomy, and were Luke (the author of Acts) to have learned of it, he would have rejected it. In Acts, being Christian is by its very nature a public confession and identity. In fact, the very word *Christian* (*Christianos* in Greek and *Christianus* in Latin) is a public word. Contrary to what we might normally think, *Christian* was not first used as an internal self-designation. It was instead a term coined by outsiders, by those who could see a thriving community and needed a word with which to describe them (see Acts 11:26, 26:28, and 1 Peter 4:16). To be a "Christian" was to belong to a group whose life was publicly visible.

One of the more obvious and important ways Acts evinces the public nature of the thriving community of early Christians is through

Luke's consistent portrayal of the Christian community as a force for cultural destabilization in the wider Mediterranean world. In Philippi, Athens, Corinth, and Ephesus, the Christian presence is disrupting enough that the Christians are hauled before the authorities and forced to account for their behavior.

Finally, the theological language in Acts for the fact that being Christian is not a private matter is *witness*. *Witness* and its cognates occur about three dozen times in Acts. This language points ultimately to the fact that thriving Christian communities in Acts are not self-existent in either their cause (they do not replicate themselves or their own mission in the world, but God's) or their telos (their aim is not survival or even necessarily success in a directly tangible way). They exist as a witness to something beyond them. In a very deep sense, this means that thriving according to Acts entails a turn away from the self, the internally focused vision that so many communities have and in which they remain caught.

3. Provision for the weak

One of the potential difficulties in describing something as "thriving" is that it can evoke images that have to do with health, strength, vitality, independence, flourishing, and so on to the explicit exclusion of weakness, sickness, and dependence. But to read Acts well is to realize that we would be deeply mistaken if we were to think of thriving solely in terms of the strong. In Acts, thriving includes provision for and inclusion of the weak and the downtrodden—not as a kind of "add-on" to the central mission of the church but as something integral and internal to its identity.

Indeed, the first real communal problem in the church—a threat to its thriving—occurs when the so-called Hellenists (Greek speakers) complain against the Hebrews (Aramaic speakers) because the Hebrews are neglecting the Greek-speaking widows in the daily distribution of provisions. Acts devotes only a few sentences to this controversy (see 6:1–6), but we know it seriously threatened the church because all twelve apostles appear on the scene, and they, in turn, summon the other leaders and develop an authority structure (deacons). By developing a lasting structure to deal with the potential rupture in the church, Acts displays what becomes a central feature of the thinking of the church's leaders: they look beyond the need to "fix" a problem (of which there are several in Acts) and instead think about thriving in a much longer-term perspective. That such a long-term, structurally focused perspective is powerfully depicted in relation to the provision for the weak should be no surprise to the reader of Acts: as Acts says explicitly in its depiction of Christian life in 2:41–47 and 4:32–37, provision for all is fundamental to the thriving of the early Christian communities.

4. Processing disagreement/conflict

If we asked enough people, we would doubtless discover a tendency to think that disagreement and conflict are incompatible with thriving. The simple reason for the prevalence of this thought is that it is at least somewhat true: a community cannot have ongoing, irate, throat-clenching fighting and thrive. But as a whole and in a deeper sense, thriving does not exclude disagreement/conflict. Instead, to thrive is to be able to incorporate conflict and disagreement into the life of the community.

There are many instances in which the author of Acts narrates the incorporation of conflict into the life of the community but none as well known as the Jerusalem Council in Acts 15, considered by many historians to be the first great church council. The issue at stake in that council was whether or not gentiles had to be circumcised to be saved (and by extension, therefore, whether they had to keep the Jewish law to effect salvation by Jesus). At this remove, it can be difficult for us to appreciate how important an issue this was to the early Christians, but it was the first real tectonic theological issue in the emerging church, threatening its unity at the core (think of Paul's vehemence in his letter to the Galatians, for example).

There are three indispensable elements to the way in which the passage shows the processing of disagreement/conflict; together they constitute a paradigmatic instance of the working of "traditioned innovation" (see "Traditioned Innovation—a Biblical Way of Thinking" in the present volume). First, there is the experience of the Spirit (Peter, then Paul and Barnabas). Second, there is the agreement of the Spirit's work with Scripture (James's citation of Amos). Third, there is a structure of ecclesial authority (James and the apostles have a kind of definitive weight in the final decision). Yet such elements are not given in a stepwise fashion, as if a community could always progress from the experience of the Spirit to the decision of the leaders. These three elements are instead indispensable parts of one complex and total picture. Precisely because Acts tells the story of the Jerusalem council by means of an interplay between them, we can conclude that all three are constitutive of the ability to incorporate deep conflict. The intertwining of the powerful work of the Holy Spirit, the prefiguring and confirming role of Scripture, and the discerning work of the community's leaders suggests, further, that where communities sacrifice one of these elements for the sake of any of the others, they will not be able to incorporate well the conflict and disagreement that will inevitably come in their life together.

5. Articulacy of belief

One does not have to read long in the book of Acts before encountering what becomes a major narrative device throughout the story: speeches. There are multiple speeches peppered throughout Acts (Peter, Stephen, Paul, James, and so on). The prevalence of speeches in Acts points to the basic importance of what we may call the articulacy of belief: the ability to say what it is that forms the core of the thriving community's existence.

In our day it is all too easy to equate articulacy with intellectual sophistication. But according to Acts, this equation would be a mistake. In Acts 4, Peter and John are taken before the Jewish authorities and asked by what name they have healed the lame man by the Beautiful Gate (Acts 3). Peter replies to their request with a short sermon. The authorities, says Acts, are stunned at the power of the sermon because Peter and John are "uneducated, common men" (Acts 4:13 RSV). The Greek here literally says "illiterate idiots" (*agrammatoi kai idiōtai*). In Acts, to be articulate is not necessarily to be sophisticated; it is quite simply to be able to say what is the ultimate reason for the community's existence (by what name it lives).

Knowing the ultimate reason for a community's existence, however, is not automatic, a given, something that magically appears in one's head upon joining. Much to the contrary, it has to be taught and transmitted. The necessity to teach the community's raison d'être is nowhere seen more clearly than in the first and paradigmatic episodes in Acts (chapters 2 and 4). Upon joining the church, we are told, the new converts devoted themselves to the doctrinal instruction (*didachē*) of the apostles. The new Christians learned, therefore, what the new life was that they had embraced, what it meant to be Christian. Here, as with the processing of disagreement in Acts 15, we can see traditioned innovation at work in bringing to life and sustaining a thriving community.

In the view of Acts, then, a thriving community is one that knows why it exists at all—the content of its being as a community—and is able to articulate to others this reason for its existence. Furthermore, it has developed ways of teaching this articulacy to the new people who join the community so that there is a transmission of and continuity in community identity and mission. It would not be too strong to say that without this transmission and continuity in identity, the community has no chance whatsoever to thrive in the long run.

6. Suffering

Once again, Acts confronts us with the necessity to expand the normal notions associated with "thriving." Typically, we would not associate suffering with thriving. If people are suffering, so our common sense would tell us, *thriving* is not the best word to describe their condition.

By stark contrast, to observe thriving communities in Acts is to see that they suffer almost from start to finish. This is true not only of the chief characters Peter and Paul—think of Stephen, the first Christian martyr—but also of the particular Christian communities scattered throughout the Mediterranean basin. In addition to overt stories that mention Christians who were in trouble or danger because of their faith (Jason in Thessalonica or Alexander in Ephesus, for example), we find remarks that simply presuppose suffering as a part of the life of Christian communities. For example, after Paul and Barnabas preached in Derbe, Luke tells us that they returned to Lystra, Iconium, and Pisidian Antioch, "strengthening the souls of the disciples, exhorting them to continue in the faith, and saying that it is through much suffering that we will enter the kingdom of God" (14:22).

To take suffering seriously as part of the pattern of a thriving community is simultaneously to see clearly that there is a sense in which thriving Christian communities consistently run the risk of being an offense to the world, a problematic thorn in its side. Acts would instruct us, that is, to be suspicious of our tendency to think that if we develop thriving communities, we will be liked, be rewarded for our work, appear attractive and exciting—or to suppose that because our community is thriving, people will want to join it en masse or come to work with or for us. Learning from Acts requires us to learn that to thrive in a Christian sense is also to provoke, to remind the world of both its brokenness and its hope.

In conclusion, to learn from Acts how to think about thriving communities requires us to nurture an imagination that tries to think about a total pattern of life. The six features identified above are not individual guarantors of a thriving community but are different strands of a unified community life whose interweaving constitutes a particular way of being in the world.

Networking—a Feature of Thriving Communities

Community without communication is a contradiction. The book of Acts makes this plain.

Our attempts to relate to other churches are often haphazard. Except for an occasional "pulpit exchange" or the joining of hands for a local good cause, many churches leave it up to the individual members to work out when and how people engage with another community of Christians.

It therefore can be quite surprising to discover that the early church was strategic. As the book of Acts shows in detail, the early Christians believed that it was necessary to create a tightly interlocking web of communities. The earliest missionaries would doubtless have taken all comers, but they focused on establishing communities in major urban centers, such as Ephesus, Corinth, and Rome, or in cities that were geographically well positioned for travel and trade (for example, Thessalonica, Philippi, Antioch). Establishing house churches in these locations allowed easy communication and movement between the various communities.

Because of the speed and ease of our own communication, we often pass much too quickly by the remarkable fact that the churches in Acts were in regular communication with one another. Frequently this connection between the churches is seen in the pauses between the main vignettes of the story, such as when Luke notes that after Paul and Barnabas established a church in Derbe, "they returned to Lystra and to Iconium and to Antioch, strengthening the souls of the disciples..." (14:21-22). But the importance of networked communication can also be made more explicit as it is, for instance, in relation to the all-important letter that emerged from the Jerusalem Council.

In a day when there was no form of communication other than the delivery of messages by physical presence (whether oral or written, someone had to take the message to where it needed to be) and when all travel on land was by foot or beast, the leaders in Jerusalem were nevertheless able to assume that their decision about the gentiles and the Jewish law would reach the tiny Christian communities scattered around the Mediterranean rim. This assumption was grounded in the practice the churches had long observed—the sending of key Christian leaders from community to community.

In this case, in addition to Paul and Barnabas, the "apostles and elders" in Jerusalem chose Judas and Silas to go to Antioch with their message (15:24-27). After delivering the message there, Judas and Silas were "sent off in peace" to those who had originally sent them. In returning to Jerusalem, these two men were strengthening the line of connection between the Christians in Antioch with those in the Jerusalem community. Paul and Barnabas then decided that they should, in turn, "go back and visit the brothers and sisters in every city where we proclaimed the word of the Lord" (15:36).

That they could not agree on whom to take is not as important as the fact that even after their disagreement, both Paul and Barnabas went to visit Christian communities and take the news (15:36-41). Barnabas sailed to the Christians on Cyprus (see 13:4-12), and Paul "went through Syria and Cilicia, strengthening the churches" (15:41). In short, without the networked life that was early Christianity, the effectiveness of the Jerusalem Council's decision in the life of the Christian churches would not have been possible.

It is no accident, of course, that the words "community" and "communicate" derive from the same Latin root (*communicare*).

Community without communication is a contradiction. The early Christians may not have formulated it in just this way, but they knew its truth. By developing and maintaining the links between their geographically separate communities, they displayed in a very practical sense their understanding that being one church required constant communication.

Indeed, establishing the language of "brother and sister" as a serious option for how to read other people—Christians across the Mediterranean, regardless of other differences—is literally inconceivable without the networks needed to sustain a common sense of identity and purpose. Networking in a serious sense does not automatically lead to a common sense of identity and purpose, but without networking it is hard to imagine that a unified identity and purpose could ever be maintained. To put it simply: as the book of Acts shows, the early church found networking to be indispensable for their thriving in the deepest sense—their ability to be Christians.

Visibility—a Feature
of Thriving Communities

Christians are those whose common life positions them for visibility in the world as a witness to Jesus Christ.

One of the most powerful assumptions in modern America is that there should be a division between public and private life. In some ways, of course, there has always been a proper sense of the distinction between what belongs between spouses, say, and what should be talked about in a board meeting. But the idea that there are separate spheres in which to live—and that things crucial to one sphere should not be inside the other—is a modern development. Such a view of how we are to live cuts much deeper than the sense of privacy brought about by propriety or just plain decency.

In the modern way of dividing life, for example, "religion" is not supposed to interfere in politics or play a part in a secular university classroom or a public school. Indeed, so widespread is this sense that religion should stay private that many people believe it is enshrined in the First Amendment to the Constitution. That this is false does not take away from the power of the perception: a controversy is virtually assured any time public officials speak openly about the practice of their faith. Religion thus comes to refer primarily to what one believes about God in one's heart or does on Sunday but not during the rest of the week. In short, the public-private dichotomy has made it possible for us to think that Christianity is what one does or says in a "personal" sphere, in private.

The Acts of the Apostles knows nothing of this dichotomy. In Acts, being Christian is by its very nature a public confession and identity. The Christians were a group whose pattern of life could be seen. In fact, the very word *Christian* was a public word. Contrary to what we might normally think, "follower of the man Christus" (the word's original meaning) was not first used as an internal self-designation. It was instead a term coined by outsiders, by those who could see a thriving community and needed a word with which to describe them (see Acts 11:26, 26:28, and 1 Peter 4:16). To be a follower of Christ was to belong to an assembly whose common life was publicly visible.

The visibility of the thriving community of early Christians is most dramatically portrayed in Acts through a series of scenes in which we see the Christian community as a force for cultural destabilization in the wider Mediterranean world. In Ephesus, for example, the Christian mission evokes a riot not because of any riotous action on its part but because an Ephesian silversmith can see the impact public Christianity will have upon his business. Because he makes shrines for the goddess Artemis, the silversmith discerns the clash between the religious economics of Ephesus and the burgeoning Christians. Conversions to the way of life proclaimed by Paul will drastically reduce the demand for shrines of Artemis. Far from being a publicly innocuous, purely "spiritual" movement, therefore, the Christians in Acts were consistently in the public eye. Indeed, in Philippi, Athens, Corinth, Thessalonica, Jerusalem, and elsewhere, the Christian presence is disrupting enough that the Christians are hauled before the political authorities and forced to account for their behavior. Simply put, this need to give account could not occur were the early Christians to believe that their faith was to be practiced in private. It was precisely because they took their common life to bear on the whole pattern of human existence that they were noticed.

The theological language in Acts for the fact that being Christian is not a private matter is *witness*. *Witness* and its cognates occur about three dozen times in Acts. "You will be my witnesses," says Jesus to the disciples in Acts' most programmatic statement, "in Jerusalem, and in all Samaria, and even to the end of the earth" (1:8). Paul's calling is consistently described as the making of a "witness" (for example, 22:15; 26:16). And the unity of the church is characterized by giving "witness" to the resurrection of the Lord Jesus (4:33)—to give only a hint of the importance the word plays in the story. As Acts unfolds, it is easy to see that to be a witness is to forgo the attempt to live privately as a Christian. Christians are those whose common life positions them for visibility in the world as a witness to Jesus Christ.

The language of *witness* points ultimately to the fact that thriving Christian communities in Acts are not self-existent or self-sustaining. Their visibility, that is, has a goal and purpose beyond their own mission and success. Indeed, even though they consistently found new communities in new locations, the Christians do not exist to replicate themselves. Their growth, rather, is for the sake of a public witness to Jesus Christ. In this way, Acts' story of the emergence of Christian communities in the ancient Mediterranean world argues against the modern dichotomy between public and private life and challenges Christian leaders to guide their people toward a life of visible witness as a condition of a thriving community.

Room for the Weak
in a Thriving Community

In Acts, the apostles create a new church structure to address the neglect of widows, among the most vulnerable of people.

One of the potential dangers in describing communities as "thriving" is that it can evoke images that have to do with health, strength, and independence to the exclusion of sickness, weakness, and dependence. A sickly infant, for example, can be described as "failing to thrive." In its normal, everyday sense, *thriving* does not require us to include weakness within its definition.

The Acts of the Apostles would teach us otherwise. In Acts, "thriving" includes provision for and inclusion of the weak and downtrodden. Such inclusion and provision, however, is not an extension of the core mission of the Christian community. It is, rather, part of the core mission itself. As counterintuitive as it may be to us today, the meaning of *to thrive* in relation to the communities in Acts always includes weakness.

The most striking way Acts presents this is through the narration of the church's first deep communal conflict—the first real threat to its thriving (6:1-6). The conflict arose when the so-called Hellenists (Greek-speaking Christians) began to complain against the Hebrews (Aramaic-speaking Christians): "Now in these days when the disciples were increasing in number, the Hellenists murmured against the Hebrews because their widows were neglected in the daily distribution" (6:1).

17

As Acts states it, the reason for the complaint was simple: the Hebrews were neglecting the Greek-speaking widows in the daily distribution of provisions. We are not told the specific motive behind such neglect; we are given only the bare fact itself. For an ancient reader, however, such information was more than enough. Widows, as everyone knew, were among the most vulnerable of people in the ancient world. To neglect them was to neglect the lowly, a practice that runs counter to the most basic affirmations about the nature of God's kingdom proclaimed since before Jesus's birth. As Luke himself puts it, for example, in the beginning of his Gospel, the coming of God in Jesus Christ was in part to fill "the hungry with good things" (Luke 1:53).

Yet the neglect by the Hebrews was not only physically problematical. It was also an active proclamation of the lie that the Christian church is a place that has no room for the vulnerable.

Though Acts devotes only a few sentences to this controversy, we know it threatened to undermine the church because authorities of no less clout than the twelve apostles themselves are needed to resolve the problem. And the twelve, in turn, summon other leaders of the church and develop a more elaborate structure of authority—deacons. "And the twelve summoned the body of the disciples and said, '. . . Pick out from among you seven men of good repute, full of the Spirit and of wisdom, whom we may appoint to [the ministry of serving tables]'" (6:2-3). By developing an enduring structure to deal with the potential rupture in the church, the apostles display a central feature of the thinking of the church's leaders in Acts: they look beyond the need to "fix" a problem (of which there are several in Acts) and instead think from a long-term perspective about the conditions needed for the church to thrive. That such a long-term, structurally focused perspective is powerfully depicted in relation to the provision for the weak should be no surprise to the reader of Acts: as Acts says explicitly in its depiction of Christian life in chapters 2:41-47 and 4:32-37, provision for all is fundamental to the thriving of the early Christian communities.

No less significant is the connection between this scene in Acts 6 and the scene in Antioch in Acts 11. In the Antioch scene, we learn that it was in this city that those who followed the Lord Jesus were first called "Christians" (11:26—significantly, a designation given not by the Christians to themselves but by "outsiders" looking at an identifiable group). Narratively seen, the connection between the two scenes makes the point that to be part of an identifiable group called Christian is already to include the weak and vulnerable. Thriving to the point that outsiders can recognize something new and different in the world—the community called Christians—is necessarily dependent on the community's ability to create lasting structures that include the widows. To read Acts is to see clearly that the Christian understanding of a thriving community must always define "thriving" as "inclusion of the weak."

Incorporating Disagreement in a Thriving Community

The Jerusalem Council, in Acts 15, offers three indispensable elements to processing conflict in the life of the church.

If we asked enough people, we would doubtless discover a tendency to think that disagreement and conflict are incompatible with thriving. The simple reason for the prevalence of this thought is that it is at least somewhat true: a community cannot have ongoing, irate, throat-clenching fighting and thrive.

But there is also another tendency that accounts for our aversion to conflict within the church. Put plainly, that tendency is to think that the church ought to be a place where conflict is not. The church, so this tendency tempts us to believe, is a place where holiness reigns, fights do not occur, and everyone shares equally in the joy of Christian life.

In some ways, this is understandable. Christian discipleship, so Christians of every stripe have always thought, should and actually does make a difference for the life of a community or institution. Christians are supposed to grow in holiness, for example, and no amount of open-eyed and serious reckoning with the reality of sin should suggest otherwise. The problem, however, is that this aversion to conflict can all too easily overspiritualize the church and lead to a refusal to recognize its materiality, its "still-on-the-way-ness" that shows itself in everyday, real life.

In ancient terms, such spiritualizing would find its home in Gnosticism. Contrary to the promises of the popular media, there are many, many more things that we do not know about the Gnostics than we do. But we do know that their tendencies were toward the denial of sin and a consequent overemphasis on human freedom and the possibility for perfection. The Gnostics were "spiritual" people, those who thought that their knowledge of divine things would set them apart from the problems of the real, still-quite-sinful world.

The New Testament itself does not share the view of the Gnostics. Indeed, the Acts of the Apostles—often wrongly thought to smooth over church conflict—shows a church with considerable conflict and disagreement. Often, the disagreement is compressed or seen most easily "between the lines," such as in the case of Paul and Barnabas's parting (15:36-41). But the overall picture remains clear: reading Acts would teach us that thriving does not exclude disagreement/conflict. Instead, according to Acts, to thrive is to be able to incorporate conflict and disagreement into the life of the community.

The most famous example in which the author of Acts narrates the incorporation of conflict into the life of the community is the Jerusalem Council in Acts 15, considered by many historians to be the first great church council. The issue at stake in that council was whether gentiles had to be circumcised to be saved (and by extension, therefore, whether they had to keep the Jewish law to put into effect the salvation given by Jesus). At this distance from the first century, it can be difficult for us to remember how important an issue this was to the early Christians. But it was nothing less than the first real tectonic theological issue in the emerging church, and it threatened its unity at the core (for confirmation of this fact, one need only read Paul's vehemence in his letter to the Galatians, for example).

There are three indispensable elements to the way in which the passage shows the processing of disagreement/conflict. Together they display a paradigmatic instance of the working of "traditioned innovation" (see "Traditioned Innovation—a Biblical Way of Thinking" in part 3 of this volume). First, there is the experience of the

Spirit (as recounted by Peter, then Paul and Barnabas). Second, there is the agreement of the Spirit's work with Scripture (James's citation of Amos). Third, there is a structure of ecclesial authority (James and the apostles have definitive weight in the final decision).

Yet such elements are not given in a stepwise fashion, as if a community could always progress from the experience of the Spirit to the decision of the leaders. These three elements are instead indispensable parts of one complex and unified picture. Precisely because Acts tells the story of the Jerusalem Council by means of an interplay between them, we can see that all three are constitutive of the ability to incorporate deep conflict. The intertwining of the powerful work of the Holy Spirit, the prefiguring and confirming role of Scripture, and the discerning work of the community's leaders suggests, further, that where communities sacrifice one of these elements for the sake of any of the others, they will not be able to incorporate well the conflict and disagreement that will inevitably come in their life together.

Once again, the Acts of the Apostles would teach us to expand our notions of thriving. Reading Acts well requires us to include the ability to process and incorporate disagreement within the life of our churches as a mark of a thriving community. To thrive, according to Acts, is already to know that decisions of great theological weight and importance may well hang on our ability to acknowledge deep conflict and respond to its presence with discerning wisdom.

Why Does
Your Community Exist?

A community can thrive over time only if its members know why it exists and can communicate that with others.

Our dominant forms of media have changed the way we communicate. There are many ways in which these changes enhance our ability to become the kind of communities and institutions that matter for our world. We are now better enabled, for example, to develop networks across time and space that help to deepen and even extend the sense that Christians are united with one another across the globe in a common identity, mission, and hope.

There are also profound downsides to the dominant media—the practice of hurried reading, the shortening of the attention span, and the sense of isolation and loneliness that can grow from confusing electronic correspondence with palpable human presence (to name only a few of the more obvious ones). One of the risks from our current way of communicating that should most concern Christian leaders is the potential of losing the ability to be articulate.

One does not have to read long in the book of Acts before encountering what becomes a major narrative device throughout the story: speeches. There are speeches peppered throughout Acts (by Peter, Stephen, Paul, James, and so on). The prevalence of speeches in Acts points to the basic importance of what could be called the articulacy of belief: the ability to say what it is that forms the core of the thriving community's existence.

In our time it is all too easy to equate articulacy with intellectual sophistication. Those who are articulate, we tend to think, work in the university or have at least received a good education. But according to Acts, this equation is a mistake. In Acts 4, Peter and John are taken before the Jewish authorities and asked by what name they have healed the lame man by the Beautiful Gate (Acts 3).

Peter replies to their request with a short sermon. The authorities, says Acts, are stunned at the power of the sermon because Peter and John are "uneducated, common men." The Greek is more emphatic. It says they are "illiterate idiots" (*agrammatoi kai idiōtai*).

In Acts, to be articulate is not necessarily, therefore, to be sophisticated; it is quite simply the ability to say what the ultimate reason for the community's existence actually is, its raison d'être. Or, in the parlance of the immediate scene, to say by what name the community lives.

Knowing the ultimate reason for a community's existence, however, is not automatic, a given, or something that magically appears in a person's head upon joining. Much to the contrary, it has to be taught and transmitted, which is also to say learned and received. It takes time, in other words, and requires mechanisms of transmission. It cannot be sufficiently learned in the blink of the eye it takes to read an email or a text message but is instead something into which one is inducted.

The necessity to teach and learn the community's raison d'être is seen nowhere more clearly than in the first and paradigmatic episodes in Acts (chapters 2 and 4). Upon joining the church, the new converts devoted themselves to the doctrinal instruction (*didachē*) of the apostles. The leaders of the church thought it necessary to teach the fundamentals of their communal life.

And the new Christians learned, therefore, what the new life was that they had embraced, what it meant to be Christian. Here, as with the processing of disagreement in Acts 15 (see "Incorporating Disagreement in a Thriving Community" in the present volume), we can see traditioned innovation (see "Traditioned Innovation—a Biblical Way of Thinking" in this volume) at work in bringing into life and sustaining a thriving community.

In the view of Acts, then, a thriving community is one that knows why it exists at all—the content of its being as a community—and is able to articulate to others this reason for its existence. Furthermore, it has developed ways of teaching this articulacy to the new people who join the community so that there is a transmission of and continuity in community identity and mission.

It would not be too strong to say that without this transmission and continuity in identity, the community has no chance to thrive over time. And absent the articulacy of belief, the possibility of establishing and transmitting—teaching and learning—the reason for the community's existence and core mission is exactly zero.

Suffering Is Part of Thriving

If we expect to see the kingdom of God, we should expect to suffer.

To thrive is not to suffer. Such is the common wisdom. The Acts of the Apostles, however, teaches us that suffering is an integral part of the thriving Christian community. If we are to think scripturally about thriving communities, then we must expand our regular notions of "thriving."

The Christian communities in Acts suffer almost from start to finish. Shortly after they begin to preach in Jerusalem, Peter and John are brought before the leading council (Sanhedrin) to account for the ruckus that accompanied the healing of a lame man. The apostles are released, but they are ordered "not to speak or teach at all in the name of Jesus" (Acts 4:18).

As anyone familiar with the apostle Peter would know, this is something he cannot do. And, of course, he does not intend to be quiet. So again he preaches and is quickly imprisoned. Though the advice of the Pharisee Gamaliel prevents their deaths, the apostles are nevertheless beaten and ordered once again to be silent.

As the story progresses, Stephen the deacon is stoned to death by his own people, and James the brother of John is put to death by King Herod Agrippa. During his journeys, Paul is—among other things—stoned and left for dead in Lystra, flogged and imprisoned in Philippi, put on trial for his life in Athens, and nearly killed in Jerusalem by mob violence and then a secret plot on his life.

Other Christians, too, find their lives in danger. In Thessalonica, for example, Jason's house is attacked, and he "and some of the brothers" face a potential mob killing. And in Ephesus, Alexander is shoved forward into a seething mob in the theater to answer for the problem the Christians are causing the city's craftsmen.

In addition to explicit portrayals of fierce conflict in Acts, there are also statements that simply presuppose suffering as a regular part of the life of Christian communities.

After Paul and Barnabas preach in Derbe, for example, Luke tells us that they return to Lystra, Iconium, and Pisidian Antioch, "strengthening the souls of the disciples, exhorting them to continue in the faith, and saying that it is through much suffering that we will enter the kingdom of God" (14:22). If we expect to see the kingdom of God, we should also expect to suffer. A more direct statement about the presence of suffering in Christian communities would be hard to find.

Where modern sensibilities might teach us to recoil from such numerous difficulties, Acts shows that the early Christians had a much different response.

After the Christians' release by the Sanhedrin the second time, they "rejoiced because they had been considered worthy to suffer shame for [Jesus's] name" (5:41). A flogging by the Philippian magistrates leaves Paul and Silas in prison "praying and singing hymns to God" (16:23–25).

When the disciples in Caesarea do not want Paul to go to Jerusalem, where he will likely die, he responds that he is ready to "die in Jerusalem for the name of the Lord Jesus" (21:13). His willingness to go is simply an outworking of Jesus's call on his life: Jesus told Ananias that Paul would be shown how much "he will suffer for my name" (Acts 9:16), and the Holy Spirit has confirmed Jesus's words and revealed to Paul that "in every city, prison and afflictions" await him (20:23).

In short, the early Christians not only assume that suffering will be part of the pattern of their lives, they also rejoice in the occasion for such affliction—that it gives them an opportunity to witness to the Lord Jesus.

Reading Acts shows us that when we take suffering seriously as part of a thriving community, we should simultaneously see that there is a sense in which thriving Christian communities consistently run the risk of being an offense to the world, a problematic thorn in its side.

Acts would instruct us, that is, to be suspicious of our tendencies to think that if we develop thriving communities, we will be well liked, or be rewarded for our work, or appear attractive and exciting. We cannot even suppose that because our community is thriving, people will want to join it en masse or come to work with or for us. Learning from Acts requires us to learn that to thrive in a Christian sense is also to provoke, to remind the world of both its brokenness and its hope.

But all this suffering, someone might object, is the sort that has an explicit purpose, suffering that springs from the character of Christian witness. What about the sort of suffering that is not "for" anything at all, or at least anything that we can identify? Random illness, abusive violence, disasters of various kinds—surely these are not constitutive of a thriving community.

And they are not. Luke, too, knows about indiscriminate and blameless suffering, and he rejects the all-too-common notion that all suffering is somehow traceable to our sin. Some people told Jesus "of the Galileans whose blood Pilate had mingled with their sacrifices. And [Jesus] answered them, 'Do you think that these Galileans were worse sinners than all the other Galileans, because they suffered thus?'" His answer was unequivocal: "No." So, too, "those eighteen upon whom the tower in Siloam fell and killed them, do you think that they were worse offenders than all the others who dwelt in Jerusalem?" No, Jesus said, they were not (Luke 13:1–5).

As Jesus's teaching shows, suffering of this sort is not constitutive of a thriving community. But it is an indelible part of life this side of the end. The question put to thriving communities in light of the givenness of this kind of suffering is less, Why does this happen? than, How shall we respond?

In his book that reflects on the theological questions embedded in the effects of the disastrous Asian tsunami of 2004, David Bentley Hart observes that proper Christian theology does not believe that all suffering serves some larger purpose of God—that the world as we find it is the best of all possible worlds and that all things fit into some larger sublime plan.

To the contrary, says Hart, "God will not unite all of history's many strands in one great synthesis, but will judge much of history false and damnable; . . . he will not simply reveal the sublime logic of fallen nature, but will strike off the fetters in which creation languishes; and . . . rather than showing us how the tears of a small girl suffering in the dark were necessary for the building of the Kingdom, he will instead raise her up and wipe away all tears from her eyes."[1]

Hart's argument in this book should be read by all Christians who think about suffering. It is a crucially important and theologically profound corrective to the shallow or sentimental prattle we usually encounter in the face of overwhelming sorrow.

Though it does not use Hart's terms, the book of Acts illustrates a lived version of Hart's response to the world that brings us suffering. Acts portrays Christian communities that thrive despite suffering—not because of an affirmation of the meaningfulness of all difficulty but because of the hope they know from the pattern of Jesus's life.

One may well be innocent and still wind up tortured and dead (Luke 23:4, 33; Acts 23:29; 25:18-19; 26:31-32; 20:25, 38). In the face of this truth, there remains the steadfast hope of resurrection. Jesus, that is to say, was both crucified and raised.

And that is, after all, why suffering is ultimately an indispensable part of Christian community: it was part of Jesus's own existence. We follow in his pattern, Acts teaches, insofar as we exist in the reality of crucifixion and hold fast to the hope of resurrection.

Part 2

Christian Leadership

Humor as a Mark of Life-Giving Leadership

Encouraging laughter in our institutions is not simply an effort to make people happy at work. Laughter is a sign that we refuse to give in to brokenness.

"I love to laugh, ha ha ha ha, loud and long and clear!"
(Uncle Albert in *Mary Poppins*)

Should religious leaders be funny? Often we think not.

But consider this scene from the Acts of the Apostles. While on his second trip through Troas, Paul delivers a speech at the weekly Christian gathering. Luke tells us, however, that Paul gave way to the preacher's perennial problem: a long-winded sermon. "Paul talked with them," writes Luke, and "prolonged his speech until midnight. . . . A young man named Eutychus was sitting in the window. He sank into a deep sleep as Paul talked on and on and on; and being overcome by sleep, Eutychus fell down from the third story and was taken up dead" (Acts 20:7–9).

Perhaps because we're accustomed to thinking of the Bible as a book of high religious or moral seriousness, we think it isn't (or shouldn't be) funny and often miss its humor. But there is plenty to laugh at in its pages. In this scene from Acts, for example, the story displays the comedic effects of an extremely long and boring sermon.

Luke, the companion of Paul and author of Acts, is poking fun at Paul for being long-winded.

Of course, Paul points out that Eutychus is not really dead (he turns out to be just fine). Luke's humor is not dark. But it is funny. Transpose any long-winded preacher, visualize the nodding heads and soft whistles of air from the regular congregational sleepers, watch a youth group member fall out of the balcony, and you've seen something of the dramatic power of early Christian worship! The Spirit moves so powerfully that the preacher can't shut up, the members of the congregation fall asleep, and people are actually bored (almost) to death!

Having a sense of humor is a mark of life-giving leadership if for no other reason than that laughter is theologically profound. Laughter testifies to the finitude of tears. It beckons us physiologically, spiritually—even if for just a moment—into the reality that all shall not be lost, that we shall be saved. In this way, laughter instantiates hope.

Because laughter can be both a sign and a means of hope, those who believe humor and seriousness are opposites have missed a large part of laughter's importance. Laughter is, in fact, quite serious: it is a primary way that human beings—uniquely, so far as we know, among the animals—proclaim the victory of life, utter forth joy in the face of suffering and death, and offer foretastes of the time when every tear shall be wiped away. As the psalmist once put it, laughing and shouting for joy is what we'll do when the weeping is finally finished: "When the Lord restored the fortunes of Zion, we were like those who dream. Then our mouth was filled with laughter, and our tongue with shouts of joy. . . . May those who sow in tears reap with shouts of joy. Those who go out weeping, bearing the seed for sowing, shall come home with shouts of joy" (Psalm 126:1-2, 5-6).

In short, laughter is the difference between life and death. Its seriousness is its refusal to give in to brokenness and its stubborn insistence on joy as the final reality of the world.

For this reason, much is at stake in whether we laugh. To be sure, like all good gifts, laughter can be used cruelly or can function as a sign of our existential anxiety (people have been known, of course, to break into laughter at terribly sad news) or can show relief at the fact that someone else has gotten what might have been ours ("Thank goodness!" we think. "The joke's on him").

But to exist without humor is in the end to deny the hope we have been given and to turn toward death. Institutions and their leaders, therefore, who exist without laughter are on a deathward trajectory. They are, at best, anemic, hungry, and weak creatures on the way to spiritual starvation in the absence of true joy.

By contrast, institutions and their leaders who have learned to laugh—perhaps especially at their own foibles and flops—exhibit the joy that lies at the heart of the world. These leaders hold out for something better than what usually comes across the desk or explodes in a committee meeting. They know, in brief, that resurrection comes after crucifixion and life after death. And they can thus laugh—loud and long and clear.

Becoming a Christ-Shaped Leader

Christ-shaped leadership is about developing a fundamentally Christian background in your institution or organization so that Christian thought and practice are second nature.

The phrase "Christ-shaped leadership" should appeal to any Christian leader. What else are we supposed to be doing as Christians if not leading in the pattern of Christ?

The trouble is that Christ-shaped leadership has been used too many times to name various techniques or spiritual attitudes—a discrete set of things to do or to feel that will enable the leader to lead Christianly. It is true, of course, that certain practices help develop Christ-shaped leaders.

But at its deepest level, becoming a Christ-shaped leader is about cultivating the right kind of background.

The psychologist William James famously described the world around us as a "blooming, buzzing confusion." A second's thought about the virtually inexhaustible and overwhelming movement of life around us at any given moment will show the aptness of James's description, at least as this vast complexity appears to the human mind.

We cannot even begin to comprehend *all* that goes on around us in even a five-minute span—the movement of molecules, the circulation of the blood, the bugs crawling, the wind currents shifting, the traffic noises, the sounds of animals or of conversation, and so forth.

Surprisingly, however, we don't regularly experience the blooming and buzzing as blooming and buzzing. Indeed, apart from conscious reflection upon the teeming mob of stuff around us, we almost never notice it. Why?

The simple answer is that we have developed strategies that help to organize our lives by means of focused patterns.

These patterns are "sense makers": they reduce the appearance of complexity by screening out certain things and highlighting others, and they make the world appear to us in specific and manageable ways—ways that make sense of the buzzing. Most often, these patterns are not "seeable" in the foreground of our lives. Instead, they form the background.

The background is what enables us simply to take for granted that we need to do X rather than Y—in this country, vote in elections, for example, to decide on the head of state rather than stage a military coup.

The reason voting makes sense is that we are shaped by a rich background of democratic concepts and practices that allow us to take for granted that voting is what we do to transfer power at the highest level. Switch the background against which voting makes sense, and the practice of voting every four years might look rather crazy.

As Barry Schwartz and Kenneth Sharpe point out in their book *Practical Wisdom: The Right Way to Do the Right Thing,* when we see a stop sign, we don't consciously think, "Hmm, what color? . . . I know! I know! That's red! What shape? Ah, octagon! Oh, yes, yes indeed, that's the thing called a stop sign." We just know it's a stop sign.

How do we know? Not, for those who remember the Platonists, because there's an eternal form of a stop sign in which this particular sign participates or to which it corresponds; nor, for those who remember the Cartesians, because "stop sign" is somehow an innate idea that comes with all human minds at birth.

To the contrary, we know it's a stop sign because of the background that makes the red octagon "make sense" to us as a stop sign. In this case, the background is formed by the way the conviction about the importance of human life gets articulated through the dense network we call basic traffic safety: the road rules, symbols, habits of driving, and educational practices that make possible the virtually instantaneous recognition of a stop sign as a stop sign.

As these two examples show, the importance of the background is quite remarkable: it structures how the world will appear to us and therefore how we will act in it. Our perceptions and practices make sense to us because they occur against a background that provides the sense they make.

Christ-shaped leadership is about developing a fundamentally Christian background in your institution or organization.

The point is to extend, deepen, or, in some cases, begin to provide the sort of structure—both interpretive and concrete—that allows Christian thought and practice to be done by habit, as second nature. They are what "make sense" to do in your institution.

What "makes sense," however, is not always easy or straightforward.

Indeed, on any account, the most arresting fact about developing Christ-shaped leadership is realizing that Jesus himself was actually killed. By all normal appearances, that is, his life's work did not end in the triumphant establishment of God's reign but in a shameful death and a scattering of his most committed workers.

In short, from the point of view of his death, Jesus's whole ministry was a failure. Of course, Christians know the rest of the story—how God raised Jesus from the dead and reversed the verdict upon his life. The resurrection validated Jesus's ministry and drew together those who had deserted him in a new mission.

But the resurrection did not erase Jesus's death as if it could be removed from memory. Instead, the resurrection incorporated Jesus's death into what became the distinctively Christian logic: Jesus was dead, but he is risen. This logic then formed the initial background of the new world the disciples learned to inhabit.

But the early Christians quickly learned that they had to say more than just the truth about Jesus's resurrection; they needed to fill in the background that would form the conceptual and practical structure of the new movement.

The Christians, that is, needed to talk about things that flowed from the truth of Jesus's death and resurrection but weren't simply repetitions of this central fact.

For example, they had to figure out what to preach, what his ministry and resurrection meant for their reading of the Old Testament (which was, of course, the only Scripture they had in the earliest period), how to configure the community that was focused around belief in Jesus's resurrection, how to handle persecution, and so forth.

Their overall attempt was to form the background of Christian thought and practice so that the things the early followers of Jesus ought to think and do as Christians would become second nature.

The New Testament shows the early Christians hard at work in developing a Christian background.

Paul, for example, regularly fought to establish several things that subsequent generations simply presupposed: that we do not earn our way to salvation by deeds of merit, that circumcision is not necessary for gentiles to complete their salvation, that Jew and gentile are fundamentally equal before God in terms of both their sin and their reception of God's justifying grace.

The author of 1 John had to make sure that his churches knew that it was crucial to believe in the flesh of Jesus. The author of 1 Peter taught how to endure persecution and that suffering and dying for Jesus was better than cursing his name (apostatizing).

The Acts of the Apostles as a whole, in fact, is a chronicle of how the early Christians formed and reformed the background that constituted the habits of their life together. Chapters 2:37–47, 4:32–35, and the whole of 15 are what we might call nutshell versions of how the early Christians sought to create the background of Christian life. These passages concisely illustrate the interweaving of Christian doctrine, particular practices of the church, and regular communal fellowship that forms a foundational pattern for Christian identity.

This pattern does nothing less than shape the intellectual and practical conditions under which Christian life will take place henceforth.

Long after the events of Acts, the church simply takes for granted what the early Christian leaders established: that to be Christian is to believe something quite specific about the significance of the death of Jesus of Nazareth (i.e., to "give testimony to the resurrection of the Lord Jesus," as in Acts 4:33), to come together with one another "in the temple," to "break bread," to "distribute to each as any had need" (Acts 2:42, 46; 4:35), and to welcome others into the fold (Acts 15:8-9, 14).

Most of our arguments in the church today, in fact, are not about whether we should or should not abandon these things but about the specifics of their recognized and enduring force: What exactly do we need to believe about Jesus to be Christians? Can we celebrate communion together if we disagree over the meaning of the breaking of bread? What does welcoming the outsider look like?

Even our arguments, that is, take place against a common background that makes the arguments themselves meaningful and worth having. Once, this was not so; this background of our life as church actually had to be created for us to assume its presence and its terms within which our debates occur.

The power of the background to shape things Christianly cannot be overestimated.

It would be hard, for example, to imagine anyone today who seriously thought that Christians, to be Christians, did not need to believe anything in particular about Jesus of Nazareth, or have some sort of community life that included some version of the Eucharist, or practice hospitality in at least some way.

What the Apostles established is now taken for granted far and wide. Christian existence has a pattern and a structure that gives it a broadly consistent shape through time and across geographical space.

Moreover—and simply put—having a Christian background makes it easier to think and behave in ways that are Christian and harder to think and behave in ways that aren't. Against the right kind of background, thinking about how to welcome the outsider, for example, will appear as natural as wondering how to hold a youth car wash, or pay the light bill, or turn a profit.

Conversely, when we act in ways that contravene the faith—systematic lying or repeated deception, say—those around us will experience, whether consciously or not, a dissonance with the overall pattern in which we work. "What?!? That doesn't make any sense" will become a natural reaction to things that contradict or undermine the Christian background that structures an institutional or ecclesial culture.

Of course, in reality we work with multiple backgrounds, and even multiple layers of these various backgrounds, which are all simultaneously superimposed on one another. We never start from scratch but always work within an inherited background of one kind or another.

Discerning what is healthy in our inherited background and what needs to be pruned away is the work of traditioned innovation (see "Traditioned Innovation—a Biblical Way of Thinking" in part 3 of this volume): we are always and simultaneously both receiving and creating the background against which we work.

This complexity makes the creation of Christian patterns of interpretation and practice difficult, and a work that requires great time and patience. Still, it is a profound illusion to think that Christians could exercise their institutional vocation apart from a background that structures their lives accordingly.

The choice between whether or not we have a background that makes sense of our lives is a false choice; we just do and will always have sense-making backgrounds.

The crucial question, therefore, is what kind of background provides the salient features needed to develop or extend Christian institutional patterns so that our work is organized Christianly as a matter of habit.

This sort of background needs to be both deeper and richer than the democratic theory and practice that underwrites voting and at least as mundane as stopping at a stop sign. This means Christian leaders will have to learn how to think about the interconnections between Scripture, tradition, and contemporary life both creatively and hard.

Though the six features of thriving communities (see "The Pattern of Life in Thriving Communities" in part 1 of this volume) in Acts, for example, should guide a leader's imagination, there are no prefabricated formulas that will lead every time and in every case to a distinctively Christian form of institutional life. This process will vary just as leaders and their institutions themselves do.

Yet there are some basic things to which we ought to pay attention, and over the next several chapters, we will consider some of the more important features of a Christianly shaped background as we seek to understand Christ-shaped leadership.

The Formation of
a Scriptural Imagination

Learning to read the Bible well and developing a scriptural way of living requires slow reading, sustained attention, and community.

Christian leaders are to lead in the pattern of Christ. In a previous reflection, I drew attention to the importance of developing a "background" so that Christian thought and practice become second nature (see "Becoming a Christ-Shaped Leader," above). Nothing is so crucially important to the Christian shape of this background as a scriptural imagination.

Since speaking of a "scriptural imagination" is not necessarily a common way to talk, however, it makes good sense to explain what we mean.

By *imagination* we do not mean so much the capacity for certain kinds of play that we have in abundance as children and often lose as we age or a distinct area or activity of the brain that corresponds to creativity, fantasy, and the like.

Imagination, rather, means more the way the total person is involved in interpreting and being in the world—the part we actively play in constructing a vision of life for ourselves and for others.

Imagination in this sense is thus not something that exists only in our heads or is used only for particular activities, such as artistic depiction; it is also practically dense, or lived. The shape of our lives both testifies to and influences the way we imagine the world, and, conversely, our imagination helps to structure the concrete patterns of daily, lived existence.

A scriptural imagination and reading well

To speak, then, of a *scriptural* imagination is to speak about the scriptural shape of a whole life, a way of being in the world that evidences a lifelong process of transformation by the power of holy Scripture.

The language of a "way of being in the world" emphasizes the point that a scriptural imagination is not simply a matter of "thinking"; nor is it only a "doing." Such dichotomies between thought and practice, in fact, hinder our ability to be scripturally shaped precisely because they teach us to conceive of our lives as divisible things.

But human lives are not divisible; insofar as they are human lives, they are unified by the thing that is the human being through time. All of our thought takes place within the lives that we live, and our practices are inseparably intertwined with the thinking that makes the practices intelligible. Scripture aims at the formation of the total pattern that is the way we are in the world—thought and practice together in one life.

Perhaps it goes without saying, but such a view presupposes the necessity of learning about Scripture—not only what is in it, of course, but also how to read it. As it turns out, however, reading the Bible well is not something that we naturally do with some ease like learning to swim or to cut our food correctly with a knife and fork. We need, instead, to learn how to read it well.

Learning how to read Scripture well implies, of course, some sort of corresponding instruction.

A remarkable passage from the Acts of the Apostles illustrates the need for guidance in the way of reading. In Acts 8, the deacon/evangelist Philip is traveling along a road running west from Jerusalem over to Gaza when he overhears an Ethiopian eunuch (a court official of the queen of Ethiopia) reading aloud from the book of Isaiah: "Like a sheep he was led to the slaughter, and like a lamb silent before its shearer, so he does not open his mouth. In his humiliation, justice was denied him. Who can describe his generation? For his life is taken away from the earth" (Acts 8:32-33, citing Isaiah 53:7-8).

Prompted by the Holy Spirit, Philip runs to join the chariot and asks the eunuch, "Do you understand what you are reading?" The eunuch's surprising reply goes to the heart of scriptural interpretation: "How can I, unless someone guides me?" He then invites Philip into the chariot with him and asks, "About whom . . . does the prophet [Isaiah] say this, about himself or about someone else?" Philip of course is eager to teach. "Then," Acts continues, "Philip began to speak, and starting with this scripture, he proclaimed to [the eunuch] the good news about Jesus" (8:26-40). Philip the evangelist becomes Philip the exegete.

In its immediate literary context, the emphasis of the passage is largely on the necessary conditions for understanding Jesus of Nazareth as the one of whom the Old Testament speaks (as well as the result of such understanding—baptism and the welcome into Christian fellowship). The eunuch, that is, does not know about Jesus and must be shown by Philip how Isaiah speaks of him. Two millennia after the Christian interpretation of Isaiah, the fact that the figure spoken of in Isaiah 53 can be read as a prefiguration of Jesus's suffering and death is unsurprising.

But in the first century, no such interpretation was available. Isaiah 53 spoke of one who was to suffer, to be sure, but that this one was Jesus of Nazareth was entirely unknown until the Christians developed their exegesis of the passage. That Isaiah spoke of Jesus in particular, in other words, was something that needed to be discovered and learned.

The larger interpretive point of the scene with the eunuch and Philip in Acts cannot be missed: we can read all day long—even the right passages—and, without instruction in how to understand what we're reading, miss what we most need to see. Or, to put it more positively, training in how to read Scripture well is a sine qua non of good reading itself.

Tools for reading well

Saying this is the easy part. The challenge lies in knowing how to do it. Particular pedagogical practices will inevitably have some differences, but almost all instruction geared toward Christian training will focus on the acquisition of tools and the development of habits.

By *tools* we principally mean learning such things as the languages in which the majority of Scripture was written (Hebrew and Greek), the most salient features of the cultures in which the various scriptural texts were composed (ancient Palestine, Babylon, or the Roman Empire, for example), the basic facts about the individual biblical books (who wrote them and when, what their most prominent concerns or arguments are, and so forth), and the manifold ways that contemporary questions relate to ancient ones.

Strictly speaking, such tools are not prerequisites for encountering God's word through Scripture—as if God's freedom to speak is constrained by our ability or opportunity to learn Greek. But these tools are a necessary part of a serious education into Scripture's depth and complexity.

Reading the New Testament in Greek, for example, not only slows one down and forces one to pay attention to every textual nook and cranny; it also opens a range of scriptural meaning that is often otherwise unavailable. The "Greek tool" does not create the meaning; Scripture is inexhaustibly meaningful, after all. But knowing Greek does allow a further and potentially more patient exploration of Scripture's inexhaustibility. Acquiring these tools and the ability to use them takes an enormous amount of time and effort, study and memory, writing and testing. It is far from easy.

The habits of reading well

Forming good habits for reading Scripture is considerably more difficult. This is so not only because habits are hard to form (or reform) but also because many of the habits needed to read Scripture well run counter to much of the way we do daily life. Though there are many candidates for mention, four in particular stand out today.

First, reading Scripture well requires us to be slow and patient rather than fast and immediate. Scripture's patterns and treasures are often seen only with the slowest, most patient engagement with the text.

If we read the Bible as we read our email or daily news, we almost guarantee a shallow and impoverished reading. Skimming emails is fine in its own way, but this manner of reading will never lead to a scriptural imagination. Of the things we do to combat our speed, perhaps nothing is so basic as study.

The French thinker and mystic Simone Weil once argued that study helps us to pray inasmuch as it helps us to learn how to concentrate our attention (an indisputable necessity—see the next point). It is no less true that study requires us to take time with the material we are to learn and to read slowly, carefully, and with considerable patience.

Second, and inseparable from the first habit, is the need to nourish the habit of paying concentrated and prolonged attention. The riches of Scripture cannot be found, let alone mined, with scattered attention (multitasking) or a short attention span (which commercials or sound bites both depend upon and reinforce).

The entire Gospel of John presupposes and requires a reader who can mull over complex images and their various dimensions of christological significance.

John 10, for example, is a long, reflective monologue in which Jesus turns the figure of sheep over and over and meditates on its christological significance: first, it is to the shepherd that the door of the sheepfold is opened. The sheep hear the shepherd's voice, know his voice, and follow him (10:1-6).

Next, Jesus becomes the door of the sheepfold; only those who enter by this door (i.e., through him) can be saved (10:7-10). Then Jesus is the "good shepherd" who "lays down his life for the sheep" and says, "I know my own and my own know me, just as the Father knows me and I know the Father. And I lay down my life for the sheep" (10:11-15).

He adds that there are "sheep that do not belong to this fold" and that he will bring these, too, "so there will be one flock, one shepherd" (10:16). Finally, Jesus concludes by saying that the Father loves him because he lays down his life and that he lays it down of his own accord and has the power to take it up again (10:17–18).

Reading John 10 well is simply impossible to do quickly. Despite the continuity in image (sheep/shepherd), the image is not simple. Rather, it requires the reader to ponder different dimensions of Jesus's significance. Indeed, the metaphors are comprehensible only on christological premises and an understanding of the church's mission.

In John 10, Jesus is both the way in (door)—which is also to say the mediator between the Father and the believers—and the leader of his followers (shepherd). His language about the shepherd's willing sacrifice and power to rise again refers, of course, to his resurrection, but such a reference is only obvious after the event itself (i.e., later in the story world of John).

So, too, only after the mission to the church has begun does it become evident who the sheep are that are "not of this fold"; they are those whom the church seeks to bring in. In short, John presupposes Christian readers who can concentrate and train their attention on the connections between what they already know of Jesus and the church and what the Gospel is trying to teach them through its imagery.

Third, we need to cultivate the habit of reading in community. The emphasis upon reading in community (or communion) has received much attention of late, but for many understandable reasons, the habit of reading alone is hard to break.

By reading alone, I do not mean as much the simple act of reading a book silently by oneself as I do the more damaging notion that reading is what occurs between a text and an individual—an individual who encounters the text and makes of it what he will in and through his individual judgments, mind, or life.

We read alone when we think that Scripture is a matter of the text and me. Scripture, however, was written both to and for Christian communities, and the theological logic of the texts presupposes a community of readers. The church is the place where reading all the different biblical texts together as one book makes interpretive sense. Anytime we read something called "the New Testament," "the Old Testament," or "the Christian Bible," that is, we are already reading inside the community that has made the theological judgment about the unity of these various texts and passed down this judgment in the form of the Bible itself.

Not only is it historically the case that we have the texts that form the Bible because the church has transmitted these texts through time, it is also the case that the Bible makes sense as one book only in one hermeneutical place: the church that has received it as its Scripture. In Christian thinking, this community includes not only those whom we now know but also the dead ("the communion of the saints").

Finally, then, reading Scripture well requires us to remember the past—habitually. With some exceptions, ours is not a culture in which historically deep memory is developed. But we are not the first to read the Bible; indeed, it has reached us only because it has been handed down from generation to generation.

Habitually attending to the past is thus not only a way to read with those whose lives have been formed by Scripture; it is also a way to understand how Scripture has shaped—or failed to shape—its readers. Habitual remembrance teaches us, in other words, how Scripture looks when it is lived powerfully and well.

A scriptural imagination is not a "thing" we possess but a whole life, so no one seminary, congregation, or workplace could alone account for a leader's transformation. A sustained induction into the lifelong practice of reading Scripture well is indispensable for those who serve the church and a gift to a world that desperately needs it.

Cultivating Resilience

Resilience in the Christian sense is not toughness. It is a lived hope, a way to keep getting up again that has its roots in God's permanent faithfulness.

In 1997 the British group Chumbawamba released the song "Tub-thumping," which went on to become an international hit. I first heard it in 2003 blaring out of a store window on Main Street in Heidelberg, Germany, where I was stunned by the number of people who were singing along.

True, English-language music is wildly popular among German adolescents, but the people I observed ranged far beyond the teenage years. Whether they could understand enough English to follow the lyrics didn't matter.

What was proclaimed loud and clear was only one simple phrase that everyone seemed to know, the refrain that keeps people all over the world coming back for more: "I get knocked down, but I get up again; you're never going to keep me down!"

Upon reflection, I should not have been surprised at all.

Getting knocked down is as basic as being human—life just does this to us—and so is the desire to get back up. The legend of the phoenix, for example, is a story about resilience: when the phoenix dies, it is reborn out of its own ashes. All human beings are knocked down, and all long to get back up.

It is therefore somewhat surprising to realize that the refrain's last line—"you're never going to keep me down!"—speaks more of a difference between people than it does of a commonality.

Indeed, the difference between those who repeatedly get back up and those who don't is exactly the difference between those who are able to lead and those who aren't. The name for this difference is *resilience*, the ability to get back up again and again and again and again. It is not unique to leaders, of course, but it is essential for long-term leadership.

Resilience isn't, however, the typical quality we ascribe to leaders. We think instead of charisma, intellectual prowess, rhetorical skill, political savvy, financial success, or something along these lines.

But in his recent book on spotting exceptional talent, *The Rare Find: Spotting Exceptional Talent before Everyone Else*, George Anders notes that one of the best predictors of effectiveness as a leader is resilience.

The problem, Anders observes, is that standard selection processes from a variety of organizations—résumé reading, interviews, and the like—tend not to ask the kinds of questions that can provide insight into a candidate's resilience. The reason is not so much because we find it hard to assess resilience but more because we didn't know that we needed to look for it.

Admittedly, resilience is not the first word that comes to mind to describe Christ-shaped leadership.

True, Jesus did get up even from the dead. But this was not resilience; it was bodily resurrection, an act of God strictly and entirely beyond what was possible for a dead man to do for himself.

On the other hand, however, the Christians in the Acts of the Apostles, Paul's letters, and many other New Testament books display remarkable resilience in the face of overwhelming challenges.

In addition to the regular, common poverty and sickness in the ancient world, the Christians faced serious division within and lethal persecution from without, major miscalculations in strategy, authority crises, apostasy, and so on.

Taken individually, any one of these features would be enough to knock one down; taken together, they show a community under repeated duress. Under such circumstances it would be all too easy for the leaders to fold or to return to normal Jewish or pagan life.

Here, instead, is how one of them typically responded: "We are hard pressed on every side, but not crushed; perplexed, but not in despair; persecuted, but not abandoned; struck down, but not destroyed. We always carry around in our body the death of Jesus, so that the life of Jesus may also be revealed in our body. For we who are alive are always being given over to death for Jesus's sake, so that his life may also be revealed in our mortal body. So then, death is at work in us, but life is at work in you" (2 Corinthians 4:8–12). In short, we are resilient for your sake.

Such resilience, however, is not an inner strength or self-confidence. Resilience in the Christian sense is a kind of lived hope, a way to keep getting up again that has its roots in God's permanent faithfulness.

When we get knocked down even to the point of death, Paul continues, we can currently keep getting back up to continue our work "because we know that the one who raised the Lord Jesus from the dead will also raise us with Jesus and present us with you to himself" (4:14). Resilience, therefore, is not synonymous with toughness. It is, rather, a response of hope.

This is important to understand because it names more specifically what we're looking for when we seek leaders who are resilient: resilient leaders are those who know the lived shape of hope. Ultimately, they figure forth the hope we have in the face of a life that repeatedly knocks us down. And in that hope, they show us what we have to cling to and thus to follow.

This is the deeper point about resilience that *The Rare Find* misses. Efficacy, fortitude, persistence, and the like are all important, but they are not finally or most deeply why we follow resilient leaders.

Whether or not such leaders are Christian, we follow them because we see in them the hope for which we yearn—or, at the very least, its shadow. Kill hope, and resilience will die with it. And where resilience is displayed, there you see hope.

But can resilience be cultivated? In many ways, it is far easier to see how resilience cannot be cultivated than to see how it can. Telling clinically depressed people, for example, to buck up or admonishing the sick or poor just to try harder produces nothing in the way of resilience or hope; in fact, it is cruel.

Still, there are at least three central ways that we can cultivate resilience. These ways of cultivating resilience emerge from the recognition of our present location within the broader Christian narrative that moves from God's good creation through the fall to the election of Israel, the redemption wrought in Jesus Christ, and the consummation of this redemption at the end.

We exist in the period after Jesus and before the consummation. In this period, God's kingdom is simultaneously *now* and *not yet* here. *Now/not yet*, that is, not only names our moment in the story; it is also shorthand for Christian knowledge of the truth about the world as we know it.

The first way to cultivate resilience within this moment of the Christian story is to recalibrate our imaginations to the reality of profound difficulty as a natural part of life.

At least in the United States, there is a pervasive sense that we are entitled to ease or at least to good things that should themselves be easy to get. The world, it is imagined, somehow owes us a good life.

The trouble, however, is that the world won't cooperate with this view and instead keeps sending us things that repeatedly knock us down. In the face of reality, we should learn to expect struggle and even gross failure (see "Failure as Christ-Shaped Leadership," below) as inexpungible patterns of human life in the world as we know it.

This is the "not yet" of Christian knowledge of the world. Perhaps surprisingly, however, changing our expectations of what the world must offer us has the potential to disclose many ways in which we already exhibit resilience in daily life—the ability to go each day to a job we'd rather not do, to face hard relationships with the hope of something better, to sacrifice our needs for someone else's sake, and so on.

Accepting the difficulty of the world allows us to note the daily forms of resilience; attending to these begins the skill of learning how to hear words of hope in the context of daily life.

The expectation of ease also has a somewhat paradoxical effect in that it can lead people to despair. When life brings nothing but struggle, then the utter lack of ease results in a kind of hopelessness—the seemingly permanent state of being knocked down.

So, second, we need to establish sites of hopefulness in the midst of despair. Here in Durham, North Carolina, the work of TROSA with substance abusers, for example, is work that teaches hope by means of focused practices of repair. In Houston, it's Pleasant Hill Baptist Church (see "Making the Connections" in this volume). And all across the nation on every single day of the week, it's Alcoholics Anonymous. This is the "now" of Christian knowledge of the world. By learning how to hope, people in despair learn how to get back up again and develop resilience step by step.

Third, as these examples indicate, resilience is best learned in community.

We often think of resilience in individual terms: this or that person is resilient. But communities of hope—the calling of all Christian communities—are actually places that have resilience written into their being. They are founded on hope, and their very existence testifies to the fact that getting back up is not simply a matter of the individual will. We can be helped back up and can learn how to help others up.

Hope too, therefore, is not only our own response to the world but is something we can extend to others and they can extend to us. Christian communities often fall far short of being places of hope, but that is their foundation and their calling.

Because of God's work in Christ, we can, quite literally, hope *for* someone else, and they can hope *for* us.

Start talking with resilient leaders and soon enough you will see that someone hoped for them in a time when they couldn't get back up. Resilience, in this understanding, is a communal practice, the fruit of a common life rooted in hope itself.

Resilient leaders are those who are best able to figure forth the hope of the community—not least in the face of failure, again and again and again.

Failure as
Christ-Shaped Leadership

Christians need leaders—and institutions—to train us in how to fail.

It is stunning that books that present Jesus as a model for a CEO, lead pastor, or community organizer ever leave the shelves. After all, Jesus was killed. Moreover, his best workers abandoned him in his hour of need, left the project incomplete, and ran for the hills. What CEO wants that?

In the reflection on Christ-shaped leadership, we saw that the most startling thing about Jesus's ministry is that it ended in failure. Moreover, this failure is not the kind that we can forget or relegate to the past. It is intrinsic to Christian faith and forms an indispensable part of the distinctive Christian logic of death-resurrection, which itself is embedded in core Christian practices.

Failure is at the heart of what Christian leaders have to offer the world.

Leaders who want, therefore, to cultivate a Christ-shaped background (see "Becoming a Christ-Shaped Leader," above) must build or develop practices that teach us how to fail. Of course, in an important sense, the tradition of "confessing our sins" in worship is the practice of failure par excellence: we learn from regular confession that the rhythm of human life entails repeated, ineradicable failure before God and neighbor. We do not confess once and for all but repeatedly—week after week after week.

Yet we need to do considerably more than rely on worship settings or confessionals alone. We must think about inscribing the reality of unavoidable failure into the DNA of our institutions.

From the medical world, for example, consider the practice of weekly M&M—morbidity and mortality—conferences at academic hospitals around the United States. In these gatherings, physicians candidly discuss their failures. There are no reporters and no lawyers involved. The speech is frank talk about the fallibility of the past week—surgical mistakes, trauma-care misfires, basic errors of judgment, and the like.

Such fallibility is not treated informally, as if the surgeons were gathered for a cup of coffee, but is instead processed corporately and with professional accountability. Cases are presented, questions are asked, responsibility is assumed, and efforts to eliminate the cause of error are made.

Of course, there are those who question the overall effectiveness of these meetings. But as Atul Gawande observes in his book *Complications*, "The very existence of the M&M, its place on the weekly schedule, amounts to an acknowledgment that mistakes are an inevitable part of medicine."[1]

The M&M conferences, that is, institutionalize the recognition of failure as something that is intrinsic to medical work. Doctors are not simply left on their own to develop a sense of their individual successes and mistakes; they are actively taught that their profession is one that regularly fails.

Christ-shaped leadership should recognize the necessity of practices, such as the M&M conferences, that routinely acknowledge the reality of failure. Yet unlike the M&M conferences, which address failure in only one significant area of life, Christian practices that teach us how to fail will need to reach much further.

This is so not only because we must address the reality of nonculpable failure—we frequently fail not because of moral or avoidable technical error but because things out of our control just "go wrong." It is also because Christianity is a total way of life, whereas medicine is not. Christians therefore need to think of failure as intrinsic to life, not simply to this or that sphere of action.

Precisely because failure covers the whole range of life, it is hard to name particular practices that we should develop to teach us about failure. But three essential practices must be in place for us to learn about failure.

The first is forgiveness. It may seem strange to say that forgiveness precedes failure, but it is the truth. In a very deep sense, the degree to which we admit failure depends upon the degree to which we already know we will be forgiven.

As sociologist Charles Bosk says in his book *Forgive and Remember*, about the way medical culture deals with error, "It is undeniable that a 'name, blame, and shame culture' discourages an open discussion of error."[2]

Indeed, the absence of forgiveness can create a debilitating sense of the need to cover up failure or reduce its effects. Why? Because without forgiveness, we are afraid of what will happen when we tell the truth about failure. Failure without forgiveness frightens us, and in our fear we learn to lie.

The second practice necessary to teach us about failure depends upon the first. It is the practice of truth telling. Seeing failure requires knowing the truth about things. Until we know the truth, we cannot see failure for what it is.

Think only of the way our politicians learn and then teach—both by example and by coaching—how to avoid political repercussions by avoiding the truth. Or how ministers learn to tell the story of their dying congregations in terms of cultural loss rather than facing the truth of their ineffectiveness. Or how leaders of faith-based organizations can discuss pressing stewardship issues with language that avoids the word *money*.

Knowing forgiveness as a way of life frees us to tell the truth about failure and, in turn, teaches us how to see it.

The third practice involves developing means of repair.

Forgiveness enables us to see failure and to tell the truth about it, but we still need to heal, to learn how to do better next time, and, where possible, to work toward eliminating the causes of error. Moreover, developing means of repair increases our experience of the power of forgiveness and therefore our willingness to tell the truth.

The regular meetings of Alcoholics Anonymous are an example of a type of repair. Not only do the alcoholics who attend come to a place of healing, they also learn there how to practice telling the truth in light of the deep understanding of forgiveness that grounds the entire movement.

The ritual that surrounds each instance of speaking in the meeting, for example, involves an anticipated group welcome that allows both newcomers and regulars to introduce themselves as the help-needing people they are.

"Hi, I'm John, and I'm an alcoholic" opens each person's intention to speak. "Hi, John!" comes the communal response. Imagine how "Hi, I'm an alcoholic" would be welcomed in virtually any other context, and it's easy to see how the power of the anticipated response frees the speaker to name his problem.

The Lord's Prayer closes each meeting: "Forgive us our trespasses as we forgive those who trespass against us" is part of the basic language that teaches AA members what they need to know to forgive and be forgiven, to tell the truth about their failure and to enjoy repair.

St. Paul did not know of AA, though he would doubtless have lauded its work.

He did know, however, the truth about human failure and that repair involves recognizing that God's forgiveness precedes our admission of deep damage and error.

In his letter to the Romans, Paul spends fourteen chapters of detailed instruction focused on the remarkable juxtaposition between God's action and our failure: "While we were still weak, at just the right time, Christ died for the ungodly. . . . God demonstrates his love for us in that while we were still sinners Christ died for us" (5:6-8).

By the time Paul gets to his central admonition to the Roman congregation in 15:7, the readers of Romans have learned that they are forgiven sinners and have received "reconciliation" (5:11). Their failure, that is, is cast in terms of God's response.

Consequently, when Paul tells them the truth about their community strife—it runs directly counter to Christian life together—they are prepared to hear it inside the welcome of forgiveness. By means of concentrating their attention on God's remarkable grace, Paul has created the space for them to tell the truth about their failure. So begins the way of repair: "Receive one another, therefore, as Christ has welcomed you, for the glory of God" (15:7).

Christ-shaped leaders must learn and teach others how to fail if for no other reason than failure will happen. It will happen because it is who we are.

But the good news is that by educating and being educated in failure, we can learn that we are already forgiven and that we can tell the truth—and we can therefore begin repair.

The world hungers for and desperately needs institutions that practice forgiveness well enough to train us in failure, that tell the truth, and that teach ways of repair. Without such institutions, it is, quite simply, difficult even to breathe.

Making the Connections

Christian leaders cannot compartmentalize their lives because Christ is the Lord of all—so all things must be seen in relation to Christ.

One of the troubling legacies left by the modern world is the overemphasis upon specialization and expertise. This may sound strange, of course, since without specialization and expertise many good things would remain missing from our lives: diagnoses and treatments of illness and disease, translations of ancient texts that exist only in dead languages, bridges and buildings that stand the test of time, and virtually countless other matters that enrich human life.

The trouble, however, is that we have become so specialized and developed such a culture of experts—witness the multitude of such people on any news outlet—that we have largely forgotten how to think in wholes or how to see the connections between all the various strands that make up our lives.

For Christian leaders, making the connections is not an option.

Perhaps the most basic Christian confession of all is that Jesus is Lord. By this the early Christians did not mean that Jesus was one Lord among many but that he was the only one, the "Lord of all," as Peter puts it in Acts (10:36). Practically speaking, this means that all areas of life are related to him as their Lord. To become Christ-shaped leaders, therefore, is to learn how to see all things in relation to Christ.

61

As the latter part of the book of Acts tells it, St. Paul, for example, saw the connection between Roman law and the Christian mission—an unlikely pairing at the beginning, to say the least. Paul was able to work inside the legal traditions of the Romans in order to present his case before the highest officials in the east (with the hope of moving on to the emperor himself).

In this way, he was able to testify to Christ in a setting to which he would otherwise never have gained admittance. Rather than simply accepting or rejecting Roman legal authority on its own terms, that is, Paul discerned how it was connected to Christ as its Lord: as a vehicle that could carry the apostle across the Mediterranean, establishing further connections to Christian communities and providing the chance for Paul to speak about Christ in unlikely places.

Or again, in 1 Corinthians Paul is at pains to show the connection between Christ and food.

Food, says Paul, is not inherently either good or evil, but it is not for this reason removed from what matters for Christian life. To the contrary, eating is a matter of Christian witness.

You cannot, Paul says to the formerly pagan Corinthians, continue going to the feasts at the temples to the gods. Such a practice challenges publicly Christ's universal lordship by displaying your ongoing allegiance to other gods (1 Corinthians 8 and 10).

Moreover, when there are those that are hungry among you, ignoring them not only shames the rich; it also flouts the most basic realities of the Lord's Supper (1 Corinthians 11).

To see food in relation to Christ is to see that how we eat is a matter of Christian witness and our understanding and reception of grace. Drawing the connection between the need of the hungry and the celebration of the Eucharist is integral to Christian life.

Admittedly, discerning the connections between things that are not normally held together is rarely easy, and even where our Christian vision is clear on one thing, it may need serious clarification on another.

In his book on community organizing titled *Blessed Are the Organized*, for example, Jeffrey Stout tells of a Roman Catholic priest whose congregation was focused on the issue of abortion but had little interest in engaging other issues of wide social import. As Stout notes, in Catholic teaching, contesting abortion is a way to work for Pope John Paul II's call to establish a "culture of life."

The priest therefore naturally agreed with his people that a culture of life could never be established while unborn children remained vulnerable in the face of political games. Yet until he was able to draw the connections for his congregation, they could not understand how a culture of life required an equally robust commitment to join the struggle against squalid poverty, violence, and political domination.

Stout observes that what was needed was the ability to extend John Paul II's call much more broadly; in short, the priest needed to help make the connections between all these things because of their relation to the one Lord of all: they are all part of the culture of life.

Christian institutional leaders regularly need to make connections conceptually, metaphorically, and institutionally. This effort creates an ecology of interdependent institutions able in partnership to do what each is unable to accomplish alone. Of the many ways in which we can learn to see the connections, three seem central.

First, as prosaic as it may seem, we need to read Scripture regularly with special attention to the astonishing array of things that we hold apart but that seem to go together for the early Christians: religion and politics, the public and the private, economics and community, body and soul, even death and life.

A prolonged exposure to the unity of life as found in the New Testament will go a long way toward disabling our tendencies to divide and compartmentalize.

Second, we need to develop a guiding image that has connection at its core and then teach this image as a way to imagine the world's connections. L. Gregory Jones has recently written of "crossing borders,"[1] and in an earlier reflection, I emphasized the importance of networks (see "Networking—a Feature of Thriving Communities" in part 1 of this volume).

But whether we think in terms of crossing borders or networks—or of the Internet or a thriving city, say—doesn't matter as much as getting clear on the importance of what the image conveys: that things are irreducibly connected, that we must actively seek out their connection, and that to miss the connection is to misunderstand the world in which we live.

Getting hold of a good image alone won't do enough work, of course. We also need to develop deeply ingrained habits of learning. But absent a guiding image, it is hard to see the telos of such habits. The image helps us to see where our habits are aimed.

Third, we need to find concrete examples of Christian leaders and communities who both see and live the connections of the world in relation to Christ's redeeming lordship.

In Houston's Fifth Ward, for example, Pleasant Hill Baptist Church exemplifies what it means to live the connections between active, traditional ministries and the fuller context of life in Houston.

Realizing, like the author of the Epistle of James, that it is difficult to call people to transformation when they have no place to live, Pleasant Hill began a community-development corporation twenty years ago that has now built hundreds of houses.

Of course, children have to be educated, and people need somewhere to go when not at home. Is this the work of the church? In the Fifth Ward of Houston, it is.

Pleasant Hill has initiated a tutoring program and supported the launch of a community center, preschool programs, and a charter school. In 2008, at a Duke Center for Reconciliation retreat with leaders of reconciliation efforts in the United States and Africa, Pastor Harvey Clemons Jr. saw the connection between the work of his church and the undocumented immigrants that were moving into communities adjacent to the Fifth Ward.

Leviticus 19:34 suddenly sprang to life—"the stranger who dwells among you shall be to you as one born among you, and you shall love him as yourself; for you were strangers in the land of Egypt: I am the Lord your God"—and Pleasant Hill began working with leading sociologists at Rice University to highlight immigration issues in Houston and beyond. In short, Pleasant Hill Baptist Church is a living example of how to discern and actively make the connections that Christ's universal lordship requires.

In an age where we take it for granted that the doctor looks at health, the engineer at buildings, the scholar at texts, the pastor at souls, and so on, we have a hard time making the connections.

But Christian leaders cannot afford to rest content with expertise and the compartmentalizing of life. Christ does not relate only to the soul or to this or that aspect of the world but draws all parts of life to himself for healing and redemption.

The failure to see the connections between the various parts of life is a failure, therefore, to discern the work of Christ—in terms of both what is already going on and what yet needs to be done.

Leadership and the Discipline of Silence

In this speedy world of words, leaders must learn how—and when—to use them.

We are awash in words. Never before in the history of the human race have so many words been so widely thrown about and with such remarkable reach. The advent of the digital age began the age of words, words, words. Of the making of books there has always been no end, but never before have we had the chance—and burden—of words 24/7/365. Email, text, Twitter, TV, and everything else. Words are always with us.

What should leaders do with words? Leaders have known from times long vanished that they need to be careful with what they say. All the ancients knew well that words *do* things. They thus educated themselves in rhetoric from beginning to end. Modern thinkers, too, have reflected on the indispensability of words, on the importance of the right words for the right thoughts, on the slippery nature of politically intentional ambiguity, and so on.

But there have also been those who have considered the danger of too many words.

In his 1851 work *For Self-Examination*, the Christian thinker Søren Kierkegaard wrote that "everything is noisy; and just as a strong drink is said to stir the blood, so everything in our day, even the most insignificant project, even the most empty communication, is designed merely to jolt the senses or to stir up the masses, the crowd, the public, noise!"

Noise.

We seem, he continues, "to have become sleepless in order to invent ever new instruments to increase noise, to spread noise and insignificance with the greatest possible haste and on the greatest possible scale." The result is that "everything is . . . turned upside down: communication is indeed . . . brought to its lowest point with regard to meaning, and simultaneously the means of communication are indeed brought to their highest with regard to speedy and over-all circulation; for what is publicized with such hot haste and, on the other hand, what has greater circulation than—rubbish!"

Kierkegaard's remedy to the noisy and speedy spread of rubbish is silence: "Oh, create silence!"[1]

There are obviously many goods to the digital age, but Kierkegaard's outburst here was far more prophetic than he would ever have been able to imagine. Perhaps the single most important thing a leader can do in a speedy world of words is to learn how to use them. In our time, this requires the discipline of silence.

If the speedy dissemination of rubbish mocks the importance of words, the discipline of silence respects their power. In a sense, silence is a prerequisite for learning how to use words well. It is often thought that silence has its roots in the importance of listening to others. This is doubtless true.

But it's also the case that the significance of silence rests in the fact that once said, words cannot be taken back. We can never *un*-say something we have said. Indeed, the political spin doctors and damage-control experts make their living off this remarkable fact about words.

We are not accustomed to thinking of leaders as those who know how to be silent. We want them to put out a statement, give a response, open the conversation, interpret the recent news, and so forth. And this, of course, is perfectly reasonable. In some ways, it is the gift and responsibility of leaders to do these things.

The trouble is that more speech sometimes turns out to be received as just more noise. And even leaders have difficulty reining in the tongue. Where we have emphasized the need for leaders to move into the digital age with ever more dexterity and speed, Kierkegaard reminds us that we should also counsel the development of disciplines that cut against the hasty production of words and more words.

Truth telling in difficult situations, for example, often requires silence. This is so not only because it can be just plain hard to get the truth out but also because it can be even harder to tell the truth wisely. Silence is the name for the time it takes to see the path of wisdom when truth is hard to tell.

The columnist David Brooks observed that the world of fast and loud often prevents us from hearing the quieter sounds from the depths. But these sounds are often those that we most need to hear when we want to tell the truth wisely.

The Epistle of James also knows the power and purpose of silence.

The author writes rather bluntly, "If anyone thinks he is 'religious' and yet does not bridle his tongue, but deceives his own heart, his religiousness is worthless" (1:26). In contrast to many other ancient writers on speech and silence, James knows that silence is the human way God's compassion is often mediated. A constant talker cannot hear the cry of the widows and orphans (1:27).

Later in the letter, the author reflects on the remarkable power of the tongue: it is like a rudder that guides a massive ship or a bit that can check a powerful steed. Used improperly, it is a match that can ignite a raging forest fire or an instrument of cursing. But properly disciplined, the tongue is nothing less than the conduit of blessing (3:1–12).

Building from James, we could say that bridling the tongue is impossible without the discipline of silence. In our time, amid the swift spread of so much rubbish, silence is something we cannot do without if we want our tongues to bless and our religion to be true. Leaders who want to speak wisely would do well to learn how to keep silent.

Christian Success

Success follows the pattern of Christ. Christ-shaped leaders include, rather than deny, the reality of failure and death.

Ah, success. Who doesn't want it?

In leaders, the desire to succeed seems to be nothing less than hardwired. Of course, some success brings with it unwanted complications—increasing busyness, for example—but by and large, the choice between succeeding and failing is not one that leaders have to think hard about.

St. Paul, for example, saw setback after setback but was indomitable in his quest to put Christian roots down throughout the Mediterranean world.

"I press on," he once said, "to take hold of that for which Christ Jesus took hold of me. Brothers and sisters, I do not consider myself yet to have taken hold of it. But one thing I do: Forgetting what is behind and straining toward what is ahead, I press on toward the goal to win the prize for which God has called me heavenward in Christ Jesus" (Philippians 3:12-14).

Part of Paul's drive to succeed in his mission was his personality. As he reminds us more than once, he was zealous well before his embrace of Jesus as the Christ. Such zealousness continued in his Christian mission—it was part of Paul's character that God continued to use.

But a more significant aspect of his resolve was his faith in God's ability to bring life from the dead. He learned this from thinking through the basic dynamic of Jesus's own life: for Jesus, success was resurrection by God from his death.

Such a view of success is not easily translatable into a formula for Christian leadership in America today.

Type into Google some combination of the words *Christian* and *success*, and dozens of pages of platitudes, drivel, and kitsch appear before your eyes. Bible verses, random "uplifting" quotations, and promises of admiration and material wealth are all put together in packages that have little or nothing to do with the historic roots of Christian faith in Jesus's death and resurrection.

Translation was not always necessary.

The early Christian martyrs, for example, knew well that they would have to die to succeed as Christian leaders. Their chief witness was their faithful perseverance in the face of certain demise. They also knew that in the eyes of the world, such success would look much more like failure.

And that is the first lesson of Christian success: it can, on first glance or to the world, look like failure.

Understandably, shutting the doors of a deteriorating church, for example, may not look like success. Yet in Christian logic, helping a dying church to die may be the only way to renewal of faith and vibrancy of life.

Seen in the logic of death-resurrection, closing the doors is not giving up hope. It is acknowledging the reality of death. To give up hope is to say that we know—above and beyond God's own knowledge—that no life can come out of that closing, that death is the final reality.

But to see resurrection is to hope that the closing of the doors will, in some strange, unanticipated—and perhaps unanticipatable—way, result in the overall giving of life to God's people. Resurrection follows death, the early Christian leaders taught the faithful.

There were other ways, too, that success took shape in the early church's leadership. These were not as obviously connected to imminent death, but they were no less important.

The church realized early on, for example, that the fledgling Christians could not sustain their new faith under the pressure of persecution simply by maintaining strong convictions on an individual basis.

The church saw, rather, that success as Christ would define it could come only by undergirding the various communities throughout the Mediterranean with structure: church leaders (bishops, for example, but also deacons), traveling missionaries that brought news from one community to another, a central locus of authority in Jerusalem that provided both pastoral counsel and doctrinal clarification, and a fully networked series of small churches (see "Networking—a Feature of Thriving Communities," above) scattered around the Mediterranean basin.

Such structure provided the way Christian leaders could nourish their new and growing family, strengthen them against both persecution and more routine difficulties, and, ultimately, enable them to develop into what became the Christian church writ large.

Much of this work was hidden, behind the scenes, but its effects are evident in the Acts of the Apostles, the letters of the New Testament, and the life of the early church in the second and third centuries.

Such hiddenness points to the second lesson of Christian success: it is not always dramatic—it may, in fact, be very slow and painful work—and many of the key players may not even be visible.

Creating lasting structures, arbitrating disputes, developing networks and the like are not inherently glorious jobs. They may never bring admiration, recognition, or material wealth.

Yet such work depends upon a robust vision for the long haul, the ability to grasp what matters most for a community's identity, and a deep understanding of the most important pressures a community will face and how to resist them—in short, exactly the kind of patient work that we should expect of leaders who guide their people toward thriving life (see "The Pattern of Life in Thriving Communities" in part 1 of the present volume) in the midst of whatever assails them.

Of course, sometimes success is actually dramatic.

In the book of Acts, for example, at Pentecost and beyond, the Holy Spirit is at work in striking and powerful ways, bringing people to repentance and dedication to the resurrected Jesus en masse, forming new communities, and creating new avenues of important work.

And that is the third lesson of Christian success: the power of the resurrection can be experienced in the midst of life now.

What sometimes looks like failure can actually be only failure to trust God to work in fresh and new ways and to embrace new directions offered to us now. To move from failure to success in such cases requires only the recognition of God's unanticipated work in the present and the freedom to follow it.

The Christians in Acts knew that Jesus's resurrection wasn't only about the future. They knew it was also about the power of the Holy Spirit in the present.

Closing the doors of the church may lead to life, but it also may be a sign of refusal to see the work of resurrection in our midst. The work of the Holy Spirit is not simply to prune; it is also to grow and to flower. The Holy Spirit works dramatically and visibly, as well as patiently, over the long haul.

The final lesson of Christian success comes from the previous reflection on failure (see "Failure as Christ-Shaped Leadership" in the present volume).

In order for Christians to succeed, we need institutions that practice forgiveness, truth telling, and repair. Such practices will teach us not only how to fail but also the specifically Christian shape of success.

By engaging in these three practices, institutions can create the patterns that allow us to learn that resurrection can follow death and that success can follow inevitable failure. And by learning the pattern of death-resurrection, we are educated in how Christians understand success.

Success, for Christians, follows the pattern of Christ: we include, rather than deny, the reality of failure and death, but we establish patterns of life that hope in, live out, and anticipate resurrection.

Listening Well

Flourishing institutions require leaders who know how to listen well, which demands the ability to pay active attention while avoiding distraction and to relate what is being said to its context.

Leaders need to know how to listen well.

It seems so obvious. Why bring it up? Because the truth is that many leaders are more focused on telling people what to do than they are on listening to them.

Admittedly, this is understandable. Much of a leader's work does turn on knowing what to do and being able to communicate that effectively. But the skill of listening is as crucial as anything else. Indeed, being able to listen well is often the prerequisite for knowing what to do. Yet cultivating the ability to listen is not something leaders tend to think about.

It is often said that listening is not the same thing as hearing.

You can quite easily, for example, hear people talk without listening to them. Words are perceived, but there is no real comprehension or effort to understand. Listening, by contrast, is much more difficult and requires discipline and effort.

Sarah Churman's moving story about entering the world of hearing for the first time as an adult provides a rich analogy for the work of listening.

Sarah was born deaf. But at the age of twenty-nine, she received a middle-ear implant that enabled her to hear for the first time. Her husband recorded the initial moments of Sarah's experience of sound, and the video has now been seen on YouTube more than fourteen million times. It has obviously touched something very deep.

What is most interesting for leaders who are trying to learn how to listen is the way Sarah describes her experience within the first weeks of being able to hear. She was completely surprised, for example, to learn that scratching her head made a noise. The crunch of croutons on her first salad in the world of sound was like fireworks to her.

The constant "internal noises"—breathing, stomach gurgling, heart beating, blood coursing through the body, and so on—were loud and obvious. The normal squeaks of her young children playing or squabbling were stunning—and miraculous. And on and on.

In short, much of the entire context of sound that remains in the background for the rest of us came immediately to Sarah's attention. Her sudden entrance into the world of sound meant that she was able to listen to things that we "hear" all the time but do not consciously acknowledge.

Sarah's attention, in other words, was immediately drawn to a more pervasive context of human life. Croutons, of course, make the same noise on the decibel scale regardless of who's listening; it was Sarah's attention and sensitivity that made them sound like fireworks.

As with any analogy, the point of connection is not perfect. Yet Sarah's story forcefully reminds us that we can develop sensitivity to a whole realm of things if we can discipline our attention.

Scripture is full of examples of leaders who listen well (and leaders who don't—think only of the various kings in the books of Kings). Perhaps the most dramatic example is the apostle Paul in his letters. Of course, Paul himself had his share of apparently tactless moments, but on the whole, his letters display a remarkable ability to listen.

Exactly how this is so is not immediately obvious. But in fact it makes great sense of one of the more initially puzzling features of Paul's letters—namely, why it is that he responds to pastoral issues with long theological discourses instead of direct advice.

Paul does give advice and direction—and outright commands—but predominately his responses to his congregations and his directions for living come through prolonged theological engagement with basic Christian claims. A chief reason for this, I have come to think, is because Paul listens well enough to hear things far beyond the direct questions or reports from his congregations and co-workers. He can therefore place the concerns of his congregations in a much wider and more meaningful context.

Think of his letters to the Corinthians, for example.

In almost every verse, these letters show that Paul is not simply answering the questions he has been asked or the reports he has heard. Instead, he pays remarkable attention to the wider civil situation in Corinth, to philosophical currents whose influence is felt in the congregation, to religious practices, to economic differences, and so on.

His sensitivity to the things of everyday life in Corinth is well honed, and he puts the sound of Corinthian life into conversation with basic Christian theology as he responds. When he deals with the church's question about eating the food that had been offered to idols, for example, he crafts a very careful response that applies the Christian understanding of worship—God alone is worthy of our worship—in a way that rules out the danger of idolatry (don't go to the temples, he tells them) but allows the eating of perfectly good food (food in itself is not idolatrous).

His reply to their question, that is, demonstrates an ability to listen to the daily workings of Corinthian life that give rise to their question even as it shows Paul's concern to engage the Corinthians with central convictions of Christian teaching. In this instance, as in many others, Paul's ability to listen enables him to tailor his response for a more precise fit.

The crucial question, then, is how we learn to listen. Perhaps the biggest obstacle to listening well is distraction. There's a sense in which distraction is obvious: even going out for lunch to talk seriously is now impossible in many places because of the TV screens that constantly clamor for our attention. Though illusions to the contrary persist, everyone should know that we cannot listen well and watch TV at the same time.

But there's another sense of distraction, one that is more active. This is the kind of distraction where we're so focused on what we're going to say next—or even on the other person's failure to understand us—that we miss what is being said; or where, in a committee meeting, we spend our energy waiting and looking for just the right moment to jump in with our personal contribution; or where, in a large gathering, we look for those whom we'd really like to talk to instead of engaging the person we're speaking with at the moment.

Eliminating or reducing distraction, whether of the passive or the more active kind, is a sine qua non of listening well.

But there are also more constructive things we can do to help us listen. I will mention three that center on developing our attention and reducing our tendency toward self-absorption.

We can, first, conscientiously structure our reading habits so that we're reading more-demanding rather than less-demanding books, essays, articles, and so forth. Contrary perhaps to initial suspicions, this is not professorial prattle. Repeated exposure to texts that demand more from us than magazines or the latest "how-to" books—or email—not only requires deeper concentration, it also exercises our attention span. In short, reading demanding material cultivates the ability to concentrate over a long period of time—the active skill of not getting distracted.

Second, we can listen to beautiful music. By beautiful I do not mean "what you like" but what is aesthetically defensible as truly beautiful. Yes, Bach and the rest.

There is no snobbery here—only the frank acknowledgment that the most technically exalted music humans produce teaches us how to listen by demanding the most of the listening act itself.

So, too, can the music of a particular people carry its voice and say melodically, hopefully, and beautifully what is much more difficult to say individually or without song.

Spirituals, for example, have long taught suffering and hope in a way that kept alive the communal memories needed to deal with past damage and to move forward in the present. Listening to them trains our attention on the experience of a people—not just this or that individual—and thereby provides the larger context in which to understand the shape that our collective history has today. Absent the sound of this context, many of the problems we now face cannot be well understood, much less solved.

Third, we can practice paying attention in silence and learn to listen to what is being said when nothing is being said.

Silence is more important to listening well than we regularly realize, and more often than not we need to be taught how to pay attention to it. Experienced pastors, for example, can help interns hear what wasn't said in the hospital room. Music teachers can help children understand the significance of the silences between the notes that must be played. English teachers can illustrate the fact that the spaces in poems are often as important as the words. Seasoned group facilitators can understand and interpret the almost inevitable sudden silences in an important meeting. And so on. Learning to listen to what is being said in silence frequently requires mentoring, an education about the kind of sound that occurs when no one speaks.

It is well known that leaders who can interpret the mission of their organization, convey a sense of why we ought to do what we need to do, and speak publicly about the significance of their work are necessary for the flourishing of any institution.

It is less well known but no less important that flourishing institutions require leaders who know how to listen well.

If it's true that listening well demands the ability to pay active attention while avoiding distraction and the ability to relate what is being said to the broader and deeper context in which the words have their significance, then it's not hard to see why flourishing institutions need good listeners.

Croutons, after all, really do sound like fireworks. But not without someone to help us listen to them.

Orienting Hierarchies toward the Good

The New Testament illustrates the wisdom of shaping a hierarchy toward a community's public witness and the importance of Christian character for leaders.

Hierarchy is a bad word for many people. What we want instead, we are told, is an egalitarian way of relating. Our institutions, our communities, our families—these should all be egalitarian. Where hierarchy issues in oppression, egalitarianism calls for mutual respect, honor, and humane treatment of the other.

Of course, Christians ought to be against true oppression and for genuine love of neighbor. But the trouble with wanting to get rid of hierarchy is that it cannot be gotten rid of.

Indeed, the very idea that we could choose either hierarchy or egalitarianism presents us with a false choice. Hierarchy is endemic to and inexpugnable from human life (at many different levels).

To be sure, the fall intensifies the difficulties we have with hierarchies (as with any part of life). But even in Eden, children would presumably have had to be raised. To believe that we could simply do away with hierarchy is akin to the idea that we could breathe air without inhaling oxygen. The question we initially face, therefore, is not, Will we have hierarchy? but instead, What kind of hierarchy will we have, and how shall it be inflected?

The difficulty is that there is no one-size-fits-all kind of hierarchy, a model to ensure that every sort of hierarchy at all times and in all places is oriented to the good. Nor is there a general rule or principle around which all hierarchies can be oriented.

Hierarchies, no less than any other indispensable form of structuring human life, are susceptible to gross evil at any time and in all places, and they likewise have the potential for being conduits of great good at any time and in all places. We cannot, then, simply say in general that one particular kind of hierarchy is better than the others.

It may well be that the Presbyterians have a better form of hierarchy than the Baptists, but the Baptists don't think so. It may well be that the Roman Catholics have a hierarchy that rankles many Protestants, but the former may in fact be better (or it may not). It may well be that the Episcopalians have tried to blend two incompatible models of hierarchy and thus failed at both. Or it may well be that the Methodists know best how to create holiness through hierarchies (or maybe not).

Who's to say, really? All the denominational hierarchies have been occasions of profound Christian witness as well as hypocrisy and failure. Laying the success and/or failure at the door of hierarchy of this or that kind proves impossible. Success and failure are more complex than the fact of hierarchy itself.

What this emphasizes, to put it rather simply, is the importance of the character of the leaders and the collective wisdom of larger communities. Scripture is full of various sorts of hierarchies (which is, of course, unsurprising if they are indelible features of life). Some show the ability to enrich life; others, to demean it.

We will take only two brief examples from the New Testament that illustrate, first, the wisdom of shaping a hierarchy toward a community's public witness and, second, the importance of Christian character for leaders within a community's hierarchical structure.

After Judas's death, the apostles decide to reconstitute the twelve—a symbol of the reuniting of Israel's twelve tribes—and they establish only one criterion: this person needs to have accompanied the original twelve as they went around with Jesus during his earthly life (Acts 1:21–22).

There were, as Luke's Gospel attests, many more than the twelve who accompanied Jesus throughout his ministry. But from these, one must be lifted up to occupy the role Judas would have played in the leadership of the early church. The wisdom here is that the original apostolic hierarchy was formed in order to display symbolically the significance of Jesus's ministry: in the life of Jesus, God is at work, fulfilling his eschatological promise to reconstitute Israel.

To lose the number twelve would be to demonstrate that God's fulfilling work was somehow compromised or perhaps even defeated. Maintaining a specific sort of hierarchy in this case is thus about the symbolic integrity of the community's witness to the significance of Jesus's earthly ministry.

The First Letter to Timothy is often maligned today by those who want it to agree with modern conceptions of equality or justice. It is true that the letter contains some difficult passages to swallow (the reading of Adam's behavior in Genesis 1–3 offered in 1 Timothy 2:14, for example), and that those who want rather simply to equate hierarchy with pernicious forms of patriarchy could find some help there for their case.

But as a whole, its specifications for leadership within the church's assumed hierarchy illustrate the truth that leadership and the moral life are inextricably bound together. Contrary to the pronouncements we frequently hear today that the "private" lives of leaders should have no bearing on their "public" role, 1 Timothy 3:1–8 insists that elders and deacons model the virtues and behaviors that work against such a separation.

For example, elders are, among several other things, not to be "recent converts." And deacons, also among several other requirements, are "to be tested." The insight behind both injunctions is that it takes time for Christian habits to suffuse one's life to the degree required for leaders. Hierarchy of the sort the church needs requires Christian leaders who evidence maturity that is visible not just "at work" but everywhere.

The wisdom here pertains to the truth that hierarchies can be poisoned by leaders whose character contravenes the mission of the community for whom the hierarchy exists. The structure then no longer helps to bear witness to the goodness of God in Christ but instead becomes the occasion for a truthful indictment of hypocrisy.

It is doubtless true, of course, that hierarchical structures can themselves be the problem and that no amount of good will or good character would be sufficient to address the systemic sin that results. In such cases, the structure itself needs to be criticized and changed. Christian thinking about hierarchy, that is, assumes the necessity of prophets.

But prophets in the biblical sense are much more than the contemporary view of them as "truth tellers" or those whose principal job is to speak "truth to power." Prophets should tell the truth, but they tell the truth for the sake of the larger community or communities to which they are resolutely committed.

As Michael Walzer has noted, they are "connected critics," those whose truth telling serves the irreplaceably important role of constructively guiding the community toward its rightful end. Prophets, in short, aim to work themselves out of a job: the prophetic vocation assumes the hope that prophets will not only be heard but also be heeded.

And what comes about after prophetic criticism and dismantling will not be "no-hierarchy" but only a different—and, one hopes, better—sort of hierarchy. When that change occurs, wisdom will be needed to identify leaders who refuse the dichotomy between public and private life and who see the possibility of Christian witness in and through community or institutional order.

In the end, talking about hierarchy thus turns out to be another way to highlight the importance of Christ-shaped leadership and thriving communities. If it is right to say that hierarchy or no-hierarchy is a false choice, then it is to our peril that we ignore hierarchy's inevitable role in our lives.

It simply will not do for Christian leaders to complain about hierarchy itself. The critical issue, rather, is how best to cultivate its potential for a community's witness to Christ in light of the leaders who inevitably shape much of its functioning in actual daily life.

Our Most Significant Experiences
Are in Institutions

Andy Crouch's recent book on power helps us understand that institutions are where Christians become Christians. And leaders, those in power, are the ones who shape institutional life.

In reading Andy Crouch's remarkable new book on power, I was stopped dead in my tracks. The reason was this: "It is within institutions . . . that our most significant human experiences take place. Institutions are at the heart of culture making, which means they are at the heart of human flourishing and the comprehensive flourishing of creation that we call *shalom*. Without institutions, in fact, human beings would be as feeble and futile as a flat football."[1]

Such a clear statement about the importance of institutions is hard to find today. Not only are institutions much maligned, even those most committed to them would hardly say that it is in them that "our most significant human experiences take place."

Yet Crouch is basically right. Of course, he defines institutions in a very broad way that includes families, sports, corporations, and so on, but even when considered theologically, his point holds true.

For after all, the Christian church is an institution. Moreover, many of its extensions—parachurch organizations, denominational bureaucracies, charities of this or that kind—are themselves institutions, too. Some Christians, riding the latest wave of anti-institutional sentiment, prefer the word "community" to that of "institution" or even "church."

But communities are really just institutions aborning (or, perhaps, a-dying), and to the extent that small communities identify themselves as Christian communities, they join hands with the larger history of the Christian church and participate in its basic patterns. Indeed, in the New Testament itself, *ekklēsia* (church) and *koinōnia* (community/fellowship) are theologically intelligible only in light of each other. Despite all the current sentiment that would say otherwise, when one thinks "Christian church" and/or "Christian community," one has to think "institutions" at the same time.

Christian institutions are where Christians are formed, where we have our most significant experiences of Christian life. This is hardly to say that we don't have significant experiences outside our Christian communities. But it is to say that the context in which we become habituated into what being Christian is turns out to be institutional. If leaders know nothing else about the power of their institutions, they should know that their institutions are where Christians become the Christians they become.

In this light, it is no wonder that the New Testament texts spend so much time trying to show who the leaders of the church are: they are those who will shape the space in which Christian formation happens. In contrast to the reluctance of many today to speak frank words about changing churches, Paul chided his fellow Christians in Galatia for their willingness to follow another set of leaders.

The Galatians' defection to the "disturbers" was tantamount to switching gospels. "I am astonished that you are so quickly deserting him who called you in the grace of Christ and turning to another gospel—not that there is another gospel, but there are some who disturb you and want to turn away from the gospel of Christ" (Galatians 1:6-7).

Paul's broader point was not that the Christians in Galatia should be loyal to him personally because he was their leader—even if "we or an angel" should preach another gospel, do not follow it, he would say—but that the gospel he first preached required allegiance in the form of community life. To leave that gospel under the influence of other leaders was to establish a community other than the Christian church.

In Corinth, Paul's opponents, the "super-apostles," as he sarcastically calls them (2 Corinthians 11:5), were not just people who tried to teach different doctrine from Paul's. They were also trying to create a different institutional pattern.

To follow them would have been to create an overall different church in Corinth (2 Corinthians 11:1–4). Paul argues and pleads with the Corinthians to stay true to the foundational pattern that would call them from sin and shape them toward holiness, to reject the teaching that would lead them astray and form them harmfully.

In Crouch's terms, the super-apostles are those who are not themselves at stake in the "institution's pain and brokenness."[2] Again, cynical readings to the contrary, Paul is not interested in personal loyalty in any kind of ego-centered way (see especially 2 Corinthians 12:19). His claims are instead rooted in the awareness that the Corinthian church will be what Christians are in Corinth. Theological truth, for Paul, is finally inseparable from the institutional pattern in which it gets expressed. The Corinthian Christians should reject the "false apostles" (2 Corinthians 11:13) not for Paul's sake but for the sake of the chance to witness to Christ in the shape of their common life.

In the Acts of the Apostles, in other Pauline Letters, in 1 Peter, and beyond, the New Testament consistently highlights the significance of the leaders who guide Christ's church. We have long known this, of course.

But what Crouch helps us understand in the wake of the last forty-five years or so of anti-institutional sentiment is in part why this is so significant. It is not only that the leaders are those who see that the truth of the Christian faith can be passed on; it is also that institutions are where Christians have their most significant experience of being Christian.

Inasmuch as the leaders of the institution are those who are the most determinative shapers of institutional life, it is they who will turn out to create the basic conditions under which we experience what it means to be Christian.

This is, to be sure, an enormous weight for leaders to carry. But there is no way to put it down without simultaneously discharging the responsibility of Christian leadership itself. It is also, however, an enormous gift, one rich with potential to use the responsibilities of power for the sake of deep discipleship and Christian witness.

"Power" in the Christian Sense Is the Concrete Shape of Hope

The work of institutions and communities will never be complete in our time. But if we live out lives of hope, we participate in God's remaking of creation in Christ.

The powerful often get a bad rap.

Given the rampant misuse of positions of power, this is of course understandable, particularly in societies where power is supposed to be diffused equally through the rule of the people. But even when we think of other ways of structuring the relations of power, it is hard for us to shake the idea that the powerful remain a problem.

Lord Acton's cliché is never far from our minds: "Power corrupts, and absolute power . . ."—you can finish the dictum yourself. But the truth is, as Andy Crouch points out in his book *Playing God*, simply saying that the wrong use of power by those "in charge" is wrong does almost nothing to help.

As Crouch suggests, "The only way to understand power's abuse is to begin with its proper use. When we begin with the best kinds of power, we learn some important truths about power that we would never learn even from the most penetrating critique. Most of all, we learn something that criticism will never teach us: what to hope for." Crouch continues: "If power is dangerous—and it is—our hearts will be most prepared to resist its dangers if they have been shaped by hope."[1]

If Crouch is right, the implication for Christian leaders is obvious: we must lead in and toward hope.

But what is real hope?

According to the New Testament, real hope is not the shallow insistence that we can make something of our own that counts. And there's a good reason for this: the truth of the human lot. Though we often refuse to look it in the face, the stark truth of our deepest trouble as leaders is something like this: all our projects will eventually fail.

Dreams may come to life, but they will die again. Good works may have lasting results, but the results will not last long enough. Buildings may be strongly constructed, but they will eventually decay and fall. "Sustainable" plans for this or that—put in the noun you like—may well get off the ground for a very long time, but they will sooner or later falter. A lifetime of work may achieve much, but it will eventually be forgotten. You may be revered and even thanked, but one day not only your work but you, too, will be forgotten.

To say it even more starkly, the trouble with leading in hope is death. For it is in fact the case that living in a world of decay and death threatens our ability to hope.

A quick glance at the New Testament's grammar of hope shows that hope is focused upon the defeat of death in the resurrection of Jesus Christ. Absent from its talk about hope is any sense that we will survive the world or that our projects will be immortal. Instead, the New Testament consistently insists that hope is in our resurrection in Christ, in what is unseen (Romans 8:24) or laid up for us in heaven (Colossians 1:5).

Hope, as Paul says, does not disappoint, but it is utterly important to know that this complete lack of disappointment comes on the other side of our deaths and not necessarily at any time before that. We can, says the author of Hebrews, be given the assurance of the things we hope for—that is faith, after all (Hebrews 11:1)—but the assurance of hope that comes with faith is the knowledge that God's defeat of death in Christ Jesus will be ours, too.

The point of the New Testament's language of hope is that hope is what Jesus Christ gives us in the face of death. Hope is not the wish that we might triumph over our most complex problems and make something fruitful that will last. It is instead the assurance that our eventual defeat on earth—and the extinction of all our efforts and projects—is in truth not the final word.

The good news is that God has already put the power of resurrection to work in present life. As the Letter to the Ephesians puts it with a startling image, not only has Christ been raised from the dead to sit at God's right hand in the heavenly places, but we, too, have been seated in the heavenly places with Christ (1:20; 2:6). This is the letter's way of saying the resurrection is present here and now in the midst of the world.

Indeed, had God not put the power of the resurrection to work in the here and now, it is hard to see why we wouldn't just wait for death and give up on the present life. The vast amount of effort and time we put into leading well would seem to be a waste.

But here is where power and hope most importantly connect. The power of resurrection that is now here is in fact the gift of hope in the midst of time. God is already making all things new. We recognize that the work is not yet complete in our time, but insofar as we live out lives of hope, we participate in God's remaking of creation in Christ.

Cultivating thriving communities and establishing vibrant institutions, for example, are the work of hope in the present. They are not ends in themselves but are signs that the proper end of human life is truly seen through the lens of hope. "Power" in the Christian sense, therefore, is the concrete shape that hope takes. Leaders who lead in power will lead their institutions and communities in the way of hope.

This short reflection has suggested that Christian leaders ought to think about power in light of the hope we have in the face of our own defeat and death. Far too often, we try to tackle the problem of power head-on with theories about this or that configuration of justice or claims that amount to little more than "you have too much power;

we want some, too." Or we simply avoid the topic and act as if Christian leaders were only "servant leaders" with no involvement in the dynamics of power.

The truth is, however, that reflecting on power is something all Christian leaders must do, if for no other reason than that they do the work of the powerful. And the way to deal well with power, as Crouch argues, is to focus upon hope. For it is nothing less than the truth of human life that all our power—and the work we're able to do with it—ends in death. And for exactly this reason, hope is what the powerful need to know most of all.

Leading in
the Age of the Image

Christian leaders must think about the place of images in their life and work, noticing that images are powerful, can be idols, and can create the space for growth in discipleship.

Our age is one of profound transitions—global, cultural, digital. We are on the move, and our daily lives are increasingly marked by significant new patterns of thinking and relating and being in the world.

There are many striking things about these changes, but perhaps none quite so striking as the role images now play in our individual and collective lives.

Reality has never before been visually shaped to the degree that it is today. Images are of unprecedented importance to our entire society, and their virtually ubiquitous reach is likewise unprecedented. Unless we intentionally get away, we are almost never outside a space dominated by images—whether that space is as small as an iPhone screen or as large as the mall or an airport.

Partly because it is a brand-new change—relative to the long view of history—and partly because it's a complex topic, we have not thought enough about the move toward a visually dominated daily life. But Christian leaders need to be thinking about images. As Rich Mouw and Andy Crouch observed in the *Seminary of the Future* report, we live in the age of visualcy.[1]

We have all seen Christianly inspired art (or at least Christian kitsch). Scenes from the Bible, doctrinal truths, liturgical practice, and so on have shaped artistic production for nearly two millennia. It was not always so.

In fact, we have no evidence of any Christian art until after about the year AD 200. And even then, the initial attempts at art were tentative or cautious—five loaves and two fish in a catacomb, a faceless shepherd with a sheep on a sarcophagus. Jesus himself was not depicted until well into the fourth century.

This overall development toward a Christian artistic culture illustrates something of its Jewish roots. With some exceptions, Jewish tradition around the time of the New Testament did not engage in robust artistic production. Most of all, Jews did not portray God. Even the gentiles knew this about the Jews: the Roman historian Tacitus, for example, notes that in stark contrast to regular pagan practice, the Jews conceive of God with their minds alone and set up no images of their God in their cities or temples. The reason for the rejection of images was simple: imaging God was a violation of the second commandment, or, more simply, idolatry.

When Christians began seriously to produce art, they did so under the conviction that in the incarnation, God had made a statement about the importance of matter. The material world could be used to depict the saving acts of God—and God the Son himself—precisely because God had assumed and redeemed human nature. The second commandment was not violated because God had imaged himself with the stuff of the created world.

Of course, Christians then vigorously debated (and frequently fought about) how best to understand such depiction: whether icons were legitimate forms of artistic representation, whether images of any kind were to be allowed in church, whether we could depict God the Father and the Holy Spirit or only the Son, and so on.

All this history evidences a thoughtfulness about the power of images that most modern Christians would scarcely understand—a deep care and concern for the way art can or cannot mediate God, for what is proper to God's nature and what isn't, for the fact that images themselves can conscript our imaginations, for the power of the everyday world of visual representation for both good and ill.

It would be too easy to offer well-known truisms about images and stop there—that women ought not to take the measure of their bodies from advertisements, that men ought not to learn what manliness is from superhuman athletes, that children ought not to be subjected to inappropriate material, and so forth.

The problem with such advice is not that it's untrue; it's indubitably true. The problem, rather, is that such advice fails to address the deeper work that images do.

A recent study, for example, found that there is no distinct area in the brain that corresponds to "aesthetics" or "art" or "images."[2] The primary area of the brain activated by the arts is, rather, the same area that lights up when we're determining what's useful for survival (what kind of food to seek, what mate to select, what's painful and what's not, and so forth).

Such a finding is profoundly important because it suggests that our response to images is in part a response to things we've learned to think we need to survive. We do not necessarily need a new shirt to survive, but precisely because images activate our sense of survival, we learn to associate them with needs as deep as survival. Therein lies both their promise and their peril. Where the need for survival is real, images lead us to life. And where the need for survival is false, images fool us and tempt us wrongly to believe that our life depends on our connection to them.

Though neuroscientific studies of the effect of images have not been around until very recently, Christians have always known that images are as powerful as our need to survive. Indeed, Paul uses the same word for image—*eikōn*—to speak both of Christ as the saving image of God (2 Corinthians 4:4, Romans 8:29) and of the idols that lead us astray (Romans 1:23). Images can tell us the truth about God and thereby connect us to the only source of life, Paul implies, and they can lie to us and lead us down the path of destruction and death.

Of course, not all images do this in an obvious or immediate sense, but life-death is nevertheless the range of their power.

The difficulty with images, then, is that their connection to our survival is both life-giving and deadly dangerous. How do we learn when it's one and when it's the other?

We learn a tradition of reflection that can catechize our imaginations. Philosophers of art such as Ernst Gombrich, as well as novelists who ponder it deeply, like Chaim Potok, tell us that there's no such thing as images without tradition. What they mean by this, in part, is that even our seeing—what we see and how we see—is learned. The rich history of Christian reflection on images cannot be learned in one day. But for leaders who must reckon with the contemporary age of the image, there are at least three things they must notice as they begin to think hard about the place of images in their life and work.

First, contrary to our contemporary sense that images are inert, Christian reflection on their power has repeatedly discerned that images are in fact more powerful than we are. They are often our masters, and not we theirs. Living in a world of images is not so much like living among things we can choose to make our own; it is, rather, more like living in a world with things that can make us their own.

Second, images can be idols, the kind that bind us to themselves and shape our lives accordingly. Swastikas and the like immediately come to mind.

But there are other, more subtle ways images seduce us and make us theirs. Take the sort of thing we see on Facebook, for example, where we can witness virtually countless posts of happy moments, milestone celebrations, and intact relationships. For such things we should give thanks, of course.

But where are the pictures of those moments when we act like idiots to our spouses or kids, shoot an air ball for the potential game winner, royally embarrass ourselves at work, enter a cancer ward, go to AA, receive devastating news, or otherwise genuinely hurt from the pain of life?

By themselves, the merry pictures combine to tell a story about human happiness that is not only false but also enticing and ensnaring. We begin to think life ought to look the way it does on Facebook. But if the Christian story is true, the story of happy moments as the full story of human life is a lie. The collage of images of only one sort finally lies to us about what kind of creatures we are and where we can put our hope.

Finally, images can create the space for growth in discipleship. It would be hard to condense aesthetics into a one-line answer to the question, What's good art *for*? But for Christians, the answer would necessarily relate to growth in our lives as Christians. (Art for art's sake is as meaningless a slogan as it is unrelated to Christian existence.) For Christians, images grow us in at least two indispensable and powerful ways.

Images have the power to tell us the truth when we'd rather not know it. It was essential, to take a well-known example, that images of the Nazi treatment of the Jews be shown in the face of unbelief and denial. With technological innovation, the manipulation of photographic images has made things more complex, of course, but the capacity of these images to tell the truth has not been weakened. More difficult to discern, perhaps, but not weakened.

The lure and importance of photographic/videographic reporting has always been to show the truth. We may not have needed images to learn that human beings will behead other human beings—the guillotine was very busy in its day—but the very fact that they can confront us in our living rooms is a forceful reminder of the human predicament and the need for Christian hope.

Images can also directly show us the work of love incarnate. The images of Maggy Barankitse and her work in Burundi in the wake of the slaughter of the Hutu/Tutsi civil war help us actually see what love looks like in the world we live in.[3] It is one thing to read Maggy's words "Love made me an inventor." It is quite another to see how love actually works. It is one thing to hear that war orphans who swim in a pool are swimming in water that cleanses their souls. It is quite another to see a cleansed soul playing in the water with joy. Images usher us into an imaginative space that gives visual shape to the truths we so desperately need to know.

Visual art engages the human being in a way that works against the common separations of modern life—between thinking and living, between work and home, between public and private.

The eminent man of letters George Steiner once wrote, "Great works of art pass through us like storm-winds, flinging open the doors of perception, pressing upon the architecture of our beliefs with their transforming powers."[4] Among other things, Steiner meant that images can transform the way we are in the world. The Eastern Orthodox Church, of course, believes that this transformational power can be known through icons. But even those who would not share this belief can understand the truth of Steiner's remark.

Images in the sense of true art participate in the transformational power of God's hallowing of creation. Even if such participation seems distant—powerfully reminding us, say, of our desperate *need* for transformation rather than its completion—the images themselves usher us into a place where our vulnerability to their power works for our good, and we begin to heal.

The Church and the Vanishing Neighbor

In the face of dramatic cultural shifts in how well we know our neighbors, one of the tasks of Christian institutional leaders will be to strengthen the role the church plays as the place where our families and distant connections come together.

Every Christian leader ought to know that the greatest commandment is to love God, and the second greatest, which "is like it," is to love our neighbor (Matthew 22:36-40; see also Paul in Galatians 5:14). Love of God and love of neighbor was the way the vast Jewish law was organized into a more basic pattern of life. Jesus, of course, knew this well and drew the connection for his audience: when you love the God of Israel, you are to love your neighbor.

The trouble is that our neighbors have vanished. We know our families, we know our co-workers, and we know our "friends" from the Internet or special interest meetings on everything from sports to fishing to favorite books to politics. But we do not know our neighbors. Or such at least is the thesis of Marc Dunkelman's new book, *The Vanishing Neighbor*.

Dunkelman argues that the social architecture of America has profoundly changed. Broadly speaking, we used to have three basic rings of relationships or connections: our families (inner ring), our neighbors (middle ring), and our distant acquaintances (outer ring).

"Neighbors" were not just those who lived near us but those with whom we could "carry on conversations about personal subjects even if they aren't entirely private: the birth of a child, for example, an ongoing illness, or a funny coincidence from a few years back."[1] Neighbors were those who knew something of our lives.

What buttressed neighborly connections, Dunkelman says, was "institutions." Whether the Elks Club, the PTA, or even the network that was the Southern Christian Leadership Conference, it was this broader institutional organization that made our connections possible and gave rise to our knowledge of our neighbors. In the days before email and all its cousins, our contact with each other was through multifaceted associations that brought us together and enmeshed us in wider, if not directly intimate, knowledge about each other's lives.

As a whole, Dunkelman observes, these institutions have all but disappeared. And with them have gone the middle-ring relationships.

It's not that we have quit caring about some of the work these institutions did. It's rather that we no longer think we need them. They have been replaced by forms of media that allow us to connect directly with those who already share our interests. No longer do we need to gather with others to pursue what we see as "good" or even just to get to know people. We simply go online, discover people who fit what we have in mind, and communicate with them about the interest or experience that led us to begin the search.

"Two people with nothing in common beyond a single point of interest can engage without worrying about other beliefs that might put them on opposite sides of a vast divide," Dunkelman notes.[2] People who share the same disease, who collect the same items, who cheer for the same college team, who support the same politicians, and so on all connect with those of like experience and thought.

To be sure, a thick network can emerge from such connections, and there is deep good in finding others who have, say, gone through the same chemotherapy. We can also achieve remarkable goals through single-minded focus: issue-based activism has never been as popular as it is now.

But over time, the dangers are that such networks become more like "networked individualism" or even "communal narcissism" than places where we know and are known.[3] And our longing for community goes unfulfilled. In fact, it actually deepens. Even the sickest want to know and be known. In Dunkelman's terms, we have loaded up on single-bond ties, or outer-ring relationships, and lost the shared sense of life that we long for.

Dunkelman doesn't really offer any "solution" to the erosion of our middle-ring ties principally because he realizes that we can't turn back the clock (and often wouldn't want to).

He does, however, recognize that without middle-ring relationships, we leave huge holes in communal life and lose the ability to integrate our lives on the basis of interpersonal knowledge and commitment. Moreover, we lose contact with large groups of people who depend on us and who may not have robust families or share our particular interests.

When a crisis comes—as it did in the fall of 2006 in Buffalo, New York, where two feet of snow caused extensive shutdown—the effect of this loss is starkly illuminated. In Buffalo, the isolation and vulnerability of a vast number of elderly people suddenly became apparent. They had almost no connection to others. Absent the middle-ring relationships, these people had been largely lost to view. That this is happening yet again in Buffalo is an indication not so much of a lack of will to help as it is once again of the fact that without middle-ring community, we cannot see our neighbors.

It would be a mistake to think that the role of the church (and/or its institutional extensions) was simply to take the place of the institutions that made the relationships of the middle ring. And yet there is a sense in which the church is still the place where the inner and outer rings come together, where our families and our most distant connections are put together through rubbing shoulders with our neighbors, and where we learn of our more immediate communal needs and opportunities. One of the major tasks for leaders of Christian institutions over the coming years will be to discover how to build ties that move beyond the immediate family and are much thicker than single-bond ties.

The New Testament churches were intertwined with a social architecture entirely different from modern America's. But we nonetheless see in them the relentless drive to connect Christians of all stripes with each other.

Christians were brothers and sisters, members of a larger networked community that imagined itself as a family. As in all families, there were fights aplenty. But the development of concentric rings of ties—from the most familiar in the household to the broadest reach of Mediterranean cities—was an indispensable ingredient in the Christian sense of identity.

Being church was not just about supporting local life in the narrower sense, nor was it simply a special interest in the way that baseball or bass fishing is. It was instead a dense and networked set of relationships that reached across the spectrum from family to neighbor to merest acquaintance to the entirely unknown brother in another place. In short, the early church was a burgeoning institution that created the connections that allowed Christians to become visible to one another across time and space.

If Christian communities are to thrive in a society that has lost its middle rings, we will have to make the connections that render us visible to one another. We cannot simply invest in our own homes and in special-interest friends.

We have no stake in renewing American middle-ring culture per se and could not do so even if we desired it. But we do have an enormous stake in knowing our neighbors and in providing the institutional space for Christians to build relationships with their neighbors—to know and be known.

Part 3

Traditioned Innovation

Traditioned Innovation— a Biblical Way of Thinking

By being both innovative and faithful to tradition, we follow the pattern of the creating and redeeming God of Scripture.

Churches, schools, businesses, families—all areas of human life—face the question of how to live toward the future in light of the past. Leaders will live out their answer to this question by the way they conceive of the world. Inevitably some will say "everything must change," and others, that "things ought to be done as they always have been." But neither is a real or even desirable option, for the world in which these pronouncements make sense does not exist.

Considered theologically, the future and the past belong together, tradition and innovation hand in hand. Traditioned innovation is a way of thinking and living that points toward the future in light of the past, a habit of being that requires both a deep fidelity to the tradition that has borne us to the present and a radical openness to the innovations that will carry us forward. Traditioned innovation names an inner-biblical way of thinking theologically about the texture of human life in the context of God's gracious and redemptive self-disclosure.

The Bible is a vast, sprawling book replete with countless winding trails. Navigating its story is best done with a compass whose points are creation, fall, election, redemption, and consummation—the theological framework in which traditioned innovation gets its meaning.

Creation

Creation is the original innovation. God begins the world's life out of nothing. Creation is thus the moment of givenness, that which provides the "tradition" upon which all human innovation is founded and dependent—the giving of life by God. We cannot make ourselves. In the face of modern claims to self-autonomy, self-made people, radical freedom from limits and the like, the book of Genesis lays bare the fact that we are always preceded. All human endeavors enter the world in a context of a fundamentally prior reality. In this sense, failure to attend to the traditions that come before us and shape us is a failure to acknowledge the depth of our dependency as created beings.

The flight from givenness inevitably involves wreckage because it wipes away an essential feature of what it means to be human. The attempt at "pure innovation," the doing away with all tradition, is ultimately an inhuman and impossible endeavor, one that shapes its practitioners and victims alike into something far less than human beings were created to be. Pure innovation simultaneously negates the givenness that underwrites human existence as such—the fact that we are here at all rather than not—and the ethical demand of this givenness: the need to recognize our historically and materially deep ties to all created life. From first to last, human beings are tradition dependent.

Fall

The narrative in Genesis of the fall powerfully illustrates that the givenness of creation is no longer simply good. It has become fractured by our refusal to acknowledge our ultimate dependency on the world God made and our attempt to become self-made creatures—as the Bible puts it, "to know as God knows." Recognizing the destruction that occurs when we deny our embeddedness in created life should cause us to be wary of attempts to dispense with everything in the past (regardless of the particular shape or kind of institution). "Everything" cannot change. We cannot rid ourselves of the world.

And yet, the fall also points directly to the necessity of innovation. Tradition is no longer sufficiently sustaining in itself. We cannot simply declare, in imitation of God's view of original creation, "this is good." And, therefore, we cannot fully rest. We must toil and move on. The character of fallen creation forces us to improvise, to try to move again within the goodness of God's originating purpose. Innovation thus becomes a necessary way of life in a world of sin and shortcoming, of brokenness and the need for new life. Adam and Eve must make their way outside the garden.

Election

The election of Abraham illustrates paradigmatically how God responds to the way we have marred the goodness of the gift. Instead of destroying his creation, we can see God's overarching response in the Old Testament in the calling of a people whose vocation is at once to embody the enduring goodness of the gift and to testify to the universal need for redemption. God does not, that is, simply scrap the world and make it all over again. Rather, God innovates. He responds to the brokenness of the world with a creative, new act—indeed, one that could not, at least on the face of it, have been anticipated from the primeval history in Genesis.

This divine pattern of innovation on the basis of tradition is repeated throughout the Old Testament, perhaps most apparently in the giving of the Torah (Law). The Torah is the defining feature of Israel's life. Israel would be indistinguishable from the nations without it. But this does not mean that the Law was seen as a static deposit of rules—a kind of inflexible, unworkable, and ultimately unlivable way of life. To the contrary, the mere existence of the book of Deuteronomy—the name literally means the "second law"—presses the point that to know the Law rightly is to grasp its fecundity for new situations. The Torah is living tradition. As even the author of Lamentations might have put it, the Law is not only tradition from of old. It is also new every morning.

Redemption

To think about redemption in the biblical sense is to see that this divine pattern of newness-without-completely-throwing-away-the-old culminates in Jesus Christ. According to the New Testament, God recreates the world in the life, death, and resurrection of Jesus of Nazareth. Those who live in the pattern of life made possible by this death and resurrection participate most fully in the newness of the world. Whoever is in Christ, says Paul, is a new creation (2 Corinthians 5:17). In Christ, that is, the innovation of God is at its peak. In Christ, he remakes the foundations of human life in the very midst of the ongoing, long-running, and everyday traditions of the world.

Yet the discontinuity—the creation of a new world—includes, rather than excludes, a continuity with what preceded Jesus. The Law and the Prophets testify to the coming of the Christ, even as that coming itself provides a new foundation on which the life promised by the Law and Prophets ultimately depends. Christ is not the "end [*telos*] of the Law" (Romans 10:4) in the sense of terminating it or displacing its reality, but is instead the deepest purpose or goal (telos) of the Law, that toward which it points or strives. In short, new creation does not abrogate the old but takes it up inside the new and in so doing remakes it. Tradition literally is made new on the basis of God's innovation.

Focusing on redemption thus discloses a productive tension that marks all life until the end. To remain in what is already known of the tradition is to refuse the priority of new creation; and yet, that which is new includes the old. Radical innovation? Yes. Radical continuity with tradition? Yes.

Consummation

Consummation points to the hope that creation and redemption will finally coincide, that the world's traditions will, as it were, catch up with the reality of a cosmos remade—that God's founding innovation and tradition will be one with his most radical innovation in Jesus Christ.

Thinking about traditioned innovation in light of the hope of consummation shows that tradition and innovation are not finally two different ways of being in the world. They are instead a helpful way to speak about the fundamental manner in which the triune God graciously relates to the world he made and to which, in the face of its profound brokenness, he remains everlastingly committed—anew. We cannot think, therefore, that tradition and innovation are opposites. In the Bible, tradition and innovation are realities of our common human life, inseparable aspects of participating in the world God made and is redeeming. Tradition and innovation go together in the divine purpose that leads toward the final restoration of God's good creation.

To the extent that we both remain faithful to tradition and innovate—even radically—we will follow the pattern of the creating and redeeming God of Scripture and will, therefore, flourish. This is not to say that the flourishing of human life will be apparent immediately to us in the present. After all, flourishing in the biblical sense is frequently counterintuitive. Israel wandered for forty years in the desert, Moses never made it to the promised land, and Jesus was killed—to take only a few striking examples. But it is to say that the underlying and ultimate purpose to which our lives will be oriented will be in harmony with the work of the God of the Bible.

Pentecost as
Traditioned Innovation

The coming of the Holy Spirit is both a fulfillment of that which is old and a radical new beginning.

Christians who hunger and thirst for change often look for inspiration to the New Testament's story of Pentecost in chapter 2 of the book of Acts. The dramatic coming of the Holy Spirit "fifty days" after Jesus's passion and resurrection signifies a break with the old way of doing things and opens the possibility of genuinely new life. Yet the newness of life after Pentecost is inseparable from the traditions that precede it, and the sustainability of such new life depends directly on the development of new traditions. To understand the significance of the coming of the Holy Spirit at Pentecost, therefore, we must hold innovation and tradition together.

During the Last Supper, Jesus told the disciples that the cup was the new covenant in his blood (Luke 22:20). After his resurrection, he instructed them to wait in Jerusalem until they received the Holy Spirit (Luke 24, Acts 1). The gift of the Holy Spirit at Pentecost is the moment at which the new covenant in Jesus Christ goes public.

Throughout the story of Pentecost, Luke draws upon a Jewish tradition that associated the feast of Pentecost (Weeks) with the giving of the Jewish law at Sinai. Knowing this allows us to see that the event in Jerusalem is narrated as the new Sinai, the new bond of God with his people on the other side of the promises of renewal heralded, for example, in Jeremiah 31 and Ezekiel 11. At Pentecost God gives "a new heart and a new spirit" (Ezekiel 11:19).

And yet precisely because the story of Pentecost cannot be told other than with the theological grammar of the Old Testament, it would be a deep mistake to see the outpouring of the Holy Spirit as an innovation that breaks fundamentally from that which preceded it. It is rather that the coming of the Holy Spirit is at once a fulfillment of that which was old—the Pentateuchal and prophetic traditions—and a radical new beginning.

The new beginning that is Pentecost runs much deeper, therefore, than a simple renewal of tradition. Fulfillment turns out to be something more like the beginning of a new age in which new communities will need to be formed. Thus does Luke interpret the coming of the Holy Spirit through the lens of the book of Joel and declare that the "last days" in which God's Spirit will be poured out have now arrived (Acts 2:16-21). And thus does Luke immediately speak of the necessity for devotion "to the apostles' teaching and fellowship, to the breaking of bread and the prayers" and the subsequent new community and its remarkable patterns of life (Acts 2:42).

This intersection of eschatological time and community life illustrates a centrally important point about life in the new reality given by the Holy Spirit: namely, that the new age, too, requires the development of tradition. In the terms of Acts, baptism must occur, apostolic instruction must be given, bread must be broken, prayers must be said, and so forth for the community to come together and grow. Absent the development of tradition, Acts would teach us, new communities risk immediate withering and extinction—indeed, decay threatens the moment after the original inspiration—for the simple reason that without the development and nurturing of tradition, a community cannot over time sustain even the vaguest sense of identity and purpose. "Untraditioned" communities—to say it baldly—do not exist. The innovation of the Holy Spirit is thus not against tradition but requires it. Fulfillment is unintelligible apart from that which is fulfilled (tradition), and life within the new reality requires ongoing organization and education in the patterns that sustain a group whose common purpose is consistently to figure forth the innovation of the Holy Spirit. More simply said, even dramatic innovation will always require tradition.

In short, it would be an ultimately impossible understanding of Pentecost to read the coming of the Holy Spirit as the new wind that blows away the stale and musty cobwebs of tradition and in their place leaves the fresh fragrance of freedom. To the contrary, in what is one of the more notable instances of innovation in the Bible, we find that the newness and freedom brought by the Holy Spirit has tradition at its core.

Navigating the Differences in the Gospels

Contrary to the message in some top-selling books, the differences in the Gospels are not a problem. Instead, they are a rich reflection of the way in which the Bible mediates God's redeeming presence to the world.

It's a sad fact that many Christian leaders no longer feel that they know how to read the Gospels. It is not their fault, really. For a long time their teachers in mainline divinity schools or seminaries did not know how to teach the Gospels. With some exceptions, New Testament professors were content primarily to point out the differences between the four Gospels. "What do you make of the fact that in Matthew Jesus apparently rides on two colts into Jerusalem while in the other Gospels he's on only one?" And they would leave it at that.

These kinds of differences between the Gospels have recently become fertile ground for spiritually deformed exploitation of our simple trust in the Gospels to tell us the truth about God and the world. In this way of thinking, the differences between the Gospels are seen only as problems, evidence of the Gospels' faulty witness. Quite naturally, of course, the Gospels are then thought to invite a thorough debunking. It is true that such books sell and make lots of money for their authors and the publishing entourage—which is all fine enough in its own way. The problem is that in the wake of poor training, this new wave of ignorance about the theological character of the Gospels looks even to Christian leaders a lot like knowledge. The upshot of this illusion is that many of us no longer actually read the Gospels to shape our thinking about Christian leadership.

But we should. If we are to think Christianly about how to practice traditioned innovation in the leading of our institutions, we could hardly find a better resource than the Gospels. Indeed, there are no texts in the Bible more important than the four Gospels. They and they alone actually narrate the life history of Jesus Christ. To read the Gospels is to become immersed in the foundational story of the Christian church and, therefore, in the pattern of traditioned innovation that sustains the church through time. How then should we think about the differences between the Gospels?

Certainly not by ignoring them or pretending they do not exist as, alas, many would evidently prefer. Indeed, any adult reader of the Gospels of Matthew, Mark, Luke, and John will notice many substantial overlaps as well as the differences among them. For example, in Matthew, Mark, and Luke, Jesus is tempted in the wilderness at the beginning of his ministry, but each Gospel tells this story in rather different ways. And in John the story does not occur at all, though a reference to it does (12:27).

At one level, the best way to explain the similarities and differences among the four Gospels is in terms of the level of a Gospel author's knowledge of one or more of the other Gospels (or knowledge of the same traditions that appear in the different Gospels). To take only two common examples, it is generally believed, first, that both Matthew and Luke used Mark's Gospel when composing their own accounts of the life of Jesus and, second, that though John was intimately familiar with many of the same basic traditions in the other three Gospels, he did not actually depend on any of them when writing his own.

But this kind of explanation of Gospel differences and overlaps only gets us so far. It does not help us understand what we are to make of the existence of such differences—the theological importance of the fact that the Gospels depend upon each other, or on common traditions, and yet go their own distinctive ways. What is the theological good toward which this reality is oriented?

If thought about carefully, the differences and similarities between the four Gospels are not obstacles to understanding them—as is frequently alleged in public or popular discussion—but are instead a rich reflection of the way in which the Bible as a whole mediates God's redeeming presence to the world. Indeed, Matthew's and Luke's use of Mark provide remarkable instances of the larger biblical pattern of traditioned innovation, the term that describes the character of God's grace as at once preserving and renewing.

In this case, certain essential elements of tradition about Jesus as narrated in Mark's Gospel—his preaching, parables, healings, friends, enemies, and so on—are both preserved in their relative order and details and simultaneously transformed by their incorporation into different narrative frameworks. Moreover, these different narrative frameworks are not simply small variations on a similar theme but are the result of artistic literary innovation. Luke, for example, is not only a scholar of tradition ("eyewitness" and otherwise; see 1:1–4); he is also a skilled writer whose theological imagination results in a new overall construal of the meaning of the life of Jesus (Gospel of Luke) and its outworking in the mission of the church (Acts of the Apostles). Luke's incorporation of well over half of Mark's text within a considerable expansion of the total picture points to the working of traditioned innovation at a deep level in the formation of the first three Gospels: the tradition is indispensable to the innovation even as the innovation extends significantly beyond the reach of the earlier tradition. Both Matthew and Luke have not only preserved but have also expanded the core of Mark's theological witness to the life of Jesus.

In the case of the Gospel of John, we see an even more radical innovation on the significance of Jesus of Nazareth. Crucial events in the life of Jesus are shifted chronologically (for example, Jesus's demonstration against the money changers in the Temple is moved from the end of his ministry to the beginning), and the theological truth about the identity of Jesus that was realized only *after* his resurrection is mediated in the Gospel narrative through Jesus's own speech *prior* to his actual death and resurrection (for example, "before Abraham was, I am"; John 8:58). Despite this narrative freedom vis-à-vis the Jesus tradition, the Gospel of John is emphatically not a gnosticizing departure from the historical figure of Jesus—a spiritualizing rumination on the secrets disclosed by Jesus's discourse with his disciples. It is instead a theologically innovative renarration of the cosmic importance of this one concrete human being. The divine Logos is the fleshly Jesus (1:14), not an abstract spiritual principle or a key to the gate of secret knowledge. As has often and rightly been noticed, John's innovative construal of the life of Jesus of Nazareth simply makes explicit what is implicit in the tradition of the Synoptic Gospels.

To read the Gospels is thus once again to encounter the biblical shape of traditioned innovation. Seen as a whole and in relation to one another, the four canonical Gospels display the reality of a living tradition and the innovations it both generates and depends upon for its ongoing transmission in the life of the church.

The New Testament as an Innovation of the Old

Understanding the New Testament requires grounding in the tradition of the Old Testament. The book of Leviticus and the Sermon on the Mount illustrate that the New is the fulfillment of the Old.

Few ideas are more incorrect in popular Christian thinking than the belief that the New Testament essentially renders the Old Testament unnecessary. To be sure, it's not usually said straight out like this. But one nevertheless can see it clearly in the common idea that the God of the Old Testament is somehow different from the God of the New (wrath vs. grace), or in vague charges of legalism slung at those who try to obey some of the Old Testament commandments, or—most prominently—in the overall failure of Christian churches to read and preach from the Old Testament on a regular basis.

In a way, these problems are understandable. Reading the Old Testament is hard work for Christians. And many leaders have much else on their plate. Still, it is literally inconceivable that the New Testament can be well understood without the Old or that Christians could develop the depth of theological leadership we need without understanding the most basic relation between the Old and New Testaments. The New depends upon the theological traditions of the Old for its innovation. The innovation, that is to say, is not against its preceding tradition but is a fulfillment of that tradition—even as it reorganizes the tradition's theological purpose around the person of Jesus Christ.

Of the manifold ways in which we could show how traditioned innovation names well the relation of the Old and New Testaments, we will focus on only two: the book of Leviticus and the Sermon on the Mount in the Gospel of Matthew.

First, Leviticus: Contrary to our initial impressions of an overly precise or even burdensome legal code, the book of Leviticus is at its heart missionary theology. It displays the intricate patterns of life that constitute the Jewish people, mark them off from the non-Jews, and, therefore, allow them to witness by their practices to their election by the God of Israel. Leviticus was, in short, a gift from God to shape the Jews into his people.

To realize that Leviticus was the fundament of Jewish practice and not casuistic prattle—as so many Christians now cannot help but take it—is to become astonished at the almost complete absence of these kinds of legal regulations in the New Testament, most especially those concerning the sacrificial cult (such as the different kinds of sacrifices we need to make, when to make them, with what animals, and for what sins). Indeed, with the exception of the theology of Hebrews, and aside from a few oblique references to sacrifice, the entire sacrificial cult is missing from the pages of the New Testament. On one level, of course, the New Testament authors simply assumed the importance of the Temple and its practices, as did Jesus himself (think, for example, of the beginning and end of the Gospel of Luke where there is a marked emphasis on the Jerusalem Temple). On another level, however, Jesus's death is interpreted as the "once for all" sacrifice (Hebrews 10:10), thereby implying that the entire cult was in a sense oriented toward this one death. Sin offerings no longer are necessary because, as the Gospel of John puts it, Jesus is the Lamb whose death takes away the sin of the world (John 1:29).

On the face of it, there is nothing in the intricacies of Leviticus, or anywhere else in the vast sprawl of the Old Testament, that could prepare for this. It is, quite simply, new.

Moreover, in Pauline theology and elsewhere in the New Testament (such as the book of Acts), the practice of the Law (Torah) no longer constitutes the primary sociopolitical or cultural boundary marker between Jews and non-Jews. Rather, being a disciple of Jesus Christ—which of course entails joining the community that takes his name—is the requisite criterion that now marks the people of God. Thus, in a two-fold and profound sense, Jesus radically exceeds the Old Testament's immediate theological range envisioned by the practice of Torah.

And yet the New Testament also claims that Jesus *fulfills* the Law and that there is no fundamental break with Jewish tradition. The transformation of Torah is hence tied more deeply to a unity in the purpose of God: to create a people who would be the light to the nations and thereby provoke them to worship the one true God. The same divine purpose that was at work in the giving of Leviticus has crystallized in Jesus. He is, as Luke formulates it both in his Gospel and in Acts, the light to the gentiles. In Jesus Christ and the community that is gathered around its devotion to him, the moment for which Torah was given and exists has arrived. Jesus Christ, as Paul says, is the telos of the Law (Romans 10:4). In this case, drastic innovation discloses the inner logic and fullness of tradition.

Second, the Sermon on the Mount (Matthew 5-7): It is often thought that the six antitheses of the Sermon on the Mount provide examples of Jesus's opposition to the Jewish law. In this common reading, "You have heard it said" is the tradition from which Jesus's innovative "But I say to you" cleanly breaks. But this is simply false. It was not against the Law to require more than the Law itself required. In fact, nothing Jesus says runs contrary to the Torah in its written or oral traditions. What then is he doing? Matthew tells us explicitly just prior to the antitheses: "Think not that I have come to abolish the law and the prophets; I have come not to abolish them but to *fulfill* them" (Matthew 5:17). The antitheses, then, actually are instances of fulfillment of the Law.

Matthew's Sermon on the Mount is paradigmatic for thinking about the link between a living tradition and the innovation necessary to keep it alive. Jesus discerned that the existing tradition ("you have heard it said") was insufficient to the task at hand; the time had changed and the tradition as it presently stood no longer resulted in the formation of "righteous" people (*righteous/ness* is shorthand in Matthew for a life of discipleship in the kingdom; 5:20). What was needed in this new time—the "kingdom of heaven" in Matthean parlance—was a move into a more radical mode of life. Only in this way could the tradition stay in step with the telos to which it was oriented: thus, *fulfillment* in Matthew means the way in which Jesus innovatively and faithfully extends Jewish tradition to accord with the change of the times—the advent of the kingdom of heaven.

King Jesus

Jesus's messianic role is bound to his identity as the son of King David. And yet, Jesus turns out to be a radically new kind of king.

Christmas is a time when we hear much about kings. The King of all was born and laid in a manger. King David was his ancestor. King Herod tried to kill the newly born King. Three other kings came to worship the true King. And so on. What we don't often hear much about, however, is the dramatic innovation that took place when Jesus was first called "king."

Israel did not always have a king. In fact, one of the more striking themes in the Old Testament is God's reluctance to allow Israel a monarch. If we follow the overall story told in the Old Testament, we are carried along in a narrative movement from an apparent anti-monarchial stance to the eschatological exaltation of the Davidic line. Through Joshua, Judges, and the opening of 1 Samuel, the Old Testament narrates on and off the reluctance of God to give Israel a king together with Israel's corresponding insistence that she have one. But after 1 and 2 Samuel's stories of the anointing/election of Saul and David, the Old Testament moves quickly to a distinctly shaped and theologically developed notion of kingship, namely, that the king should reflect the virtues of King David (read again 1 and 2 Kings).

Despite his obvious blunders, David becomes a kind of a symbol or cipher for what true kingship under God should be. By the time of the New Testament, messianic expectation included as a matter of course the conviction that the Messiah would be the son of David and would establish his kingly rule over the house of Israel (this can also be seen in certain places in the Old Testament, such as in the Psalms). In Jewish understanding, to be Messiah was to be the King of Israel. Thus it is of utmost importance to the New Testament Gospel writers not only to trace Jesus's paternal lineage through Joseph to King David but also repeatedly to portray Jesus's messianic role as essentially bound to his identity as the son of David.

Given the importance of the royal shape of messianic expectation for readers of the Old Testament—and perhaps first-century Jews especially—it would be difficult to think of a greater innovation on this theme than to say that the messianic king is not the one who has come to liberate Israel and drive the gentiles out of Palestine but is instead he who was killed at the hands of the Romans. Indeed, it is no wonder that the disciples' joyous exclamation, "Blessed is the King, the one who comes in the name of the Lord" (Luke 19:38), turns to dejection and political disappointment after Jesus's execution: "We had hoped he was the one who would redeem Israel," say the devastated disciples on the road to Emmaus (Luke 24:21). Jesus simply did not turn out to be a military monarch, a conqueror who could stun and defeat his enemies by his power. He was instead a suffering, crucified, and dead Messiah—by all appearances, a defeated king. The innovation on the theme of Davidic kingship is radical almost to the point of breaking with tradition altogether.

And yet, the very newness—even shock—of the innovation depends for its fullest meaning on a proper grasp of the tradition that constitutes the background of its radical nature. Perceiving this essential connection between the meaning of the New Testament's innovation and the tradition on which it depends prompts a careful rereading of the tradition to inquire whether it might exhibit a deeper point of contact with the innovation.

And in fact it does: God's reluctance to deal in kingship bespeaks his knowledge of the reality of monarchial violence and the way military victory might shape Israel's hopes for the future. In order to break this connection between violence and hope, the notion of kingship must be raised to its most fervent level—that of hope in military messianic deliverance—before it is shattered by the life and death of the true King. In this case, it is the radical innovation that actually creates the vision with which to see the deeper layers of God's salvific purpose in the tradition (think here, of course, of the so-called suffering servant of Isaiah 53).

To be God's true monarch, as the three kings were to see so vividly in the infant Jesus, is not to assume the mantle of might but is instead to become vulnerable, to live gently even unto death, and to trust in the hope of resurrection.

Part 4

Christmas and Easter

Why Christmas Needs Easter

The glad tidings of Gabriel, the angels, the prophet Simeon, and the others are glad precisely because the death of Jesus was not their end.

It may seem strange to suggest that part of leading well is helping people see the connection between Christmas and Easter. But it is. For without this connection, Christians have no reason for their joy. Our commercialization of Christmas tries to isolate Christmas, to make it stand on its own apart from Easter. This is a recipe only for sadness.

Of course, practically speaking, it is hard to lead when morose, and it may be even harder to follow a morose leader. More deeply, however, joy is the final response Christians can have to the world in which we live, and especially during Advent and Christmas, leaders need to understand why we can rejoice and why our institutions can be places of joy.

One of the striking things about the first Christmas is the announcement of good tidings. Of all the Gospels, the Gospel of Luke is the most explicit. The angel Gabriel says to Mary, "You will conceive in your womb and bear a son, and you will name him Jesus. He will be great, and will be called the Son of the Most High, and the Lord God will give to him the throne of his ancestor David. He will reign over the house of Jacob forever, and of his kingdom there will be no end!" (Luke 1:31–33).

Later, an angel—soon joined by "a multitude of the heavenly host"—piles up exclamations one on top of another and says to the shepherds, "I am bringing you good news of great joy for all the people! To you is born this day in the city of David a Savior, who is Christ the Lord!" (Luke 2:10–11).

And Simeon, an old prophet who was awaiting the consolation of Israel, cries out to God when he sees the infant Jesus, "My eyes have seen your salvation, which you have prepared in the presence of all peoples, a light for a revelation to the Gentiles and for glory to your people Israel" (Luke 2:30–32).

As one reads on in the Gospel, however, joy does not appear on every page.

Indeed, just as Jesus begins his ministry, he is met not by throngs of rejoicing people but by the devil, who tempts him when he is hungry and isolated. Very soon after he bests the devil, moreover, Jesus's hometown crowd first speaks highly of him but then swiftly turns on him and attempts to throw him off a cliff.

As one follows the story, demons beset Jesus, scholars challenge him, the high and mighty plot against him, and his own disciples prove hardheaded again and again. And in the end, he is executed as a criminal—in the place of the murderer Barabbas and alongside two other bona fide "evildoers," as Luke puts it.

The promised joy comes to an end. The disciples forget Jesus's predictions of being raised on the third day, and the women at the tomb are utterly dejected in their grief. Hmmm. What sort of story of glad tidings is this?

Of course, there are earlier hints that the joy will be mingled with sadness. Immediately after his prayer of thanksgiving, for example, Simeon tells Mary that her child "is destined for the falling and rising of many in Israel and to be a sign of opposition, so that the inner thoughts of many will be revealed—and a sword will pierce your own soul, too" (Luke 2:34–35).

And Jesus regularly reforms—or tries to—the disciples' expectations to include his suffering and death: "The Son of Man must undergo great suffering, and be rejected by the elders, chief priests, and scribes, and be killed, and on the third day be raised" (Luke 9:22).

Still, the promises of Christmas linger on for them; at no less significant a moment than the Last Supper itself, the disciples argue yet again about who will be the greatest in the coming kingdom—that is, they clearly still believe that Christmas is coming.

A few short hours later, however, their belief is devastated as the one who was to live out the truth of God's promises hangs upon the cross. Death, as the disciples themselves understand, is the end of these promises.

Unless, of course, death itself is overcome.

If death is no longer the end, the promises of Christmas are renewed. Christmas, in other words, requires Easter. Christmas is the announcement of glad tidings. But without Easter, Christmas is nothing but disappointment, the failed promises of God and his dead, would-be Messiah. Easter—the resurrection—is why Christmas is Christmas. The glad tidings of Gabriel, the angels, the prophet Simeon, and the others are glad precisely because the death of Jesus was not their end.

Not only does Easter resurrect the promises of Christmas (see "Why Easter Needs Christmas" in the present volume), it also transforms them. No longer can we hear Gabriel's words or the angel's proclamation without the knowledge that death and resurrection are the condition of their fulfillment. No sentimentality, no heroics, no jingle. Forward-pointing hope is what these promises become. They look to Easter for their fulfillment, and from this fulfillment comes our joy.

Many Christian institutions look for ways to acknowledge the joy that Christmas is supposed to be—churches, obviously, but also extensions of churches, such as food banks and homeless shelters, harness the "Christmas spirit" to their good ends. Leaders of these institutions would do well to note that Christmas is only the beginning, and that, in fact, were it all that we had, we would be fooling ourselves about the joy that is here.

Why Easter Needs Christmas

Remembering the story of Emmanuel at Easter helps us to remember that the way God chose to save was a way with us.

In order to retain its sense as the beginning of the good news, Christmas needs Easter (see previous chapter). Likewise, for it to retain its sense as the culmination of the good news, Easter needs Christmas.

One of the dangers of forgetting Christmas at Easter is that we tend to focus on the passion and the resurrection and forget that these are part of a larger story. We make Jesus's death and resurrection, that is, into mere events that carry with them particular benefits. So, for example, the cross is thought to cleanse us from sin and the resurrection to defeat the power of death.

Of course, Christians do believe that we are cleansed from sin and that death has ultimately been defeated. But the truth is that we cannot separate the cross and the resurrection either from each other—as if Jesus's death had specific application apart from his resurrection—or from the larger gospel story that renders Jesus's identity. They are, after all, the death and resurrection of *Jesus*.

Remembering Christmas at Eastertime helps us to realize the astounding manner by which God works redemption in the death and resurrection of Jesus. By thinking of Christmas, our attention is directed backward, from the end of Jesus's life toward its beginning.

The cross is the cross of one who was once a human baby and who went through human life and died as a grown man. The resurrection is the new life that was given to this same human being. Emmanuel, God with us, is the one who was killed and raised.

Contrary to what we might initially think, then, Jesus's death and resurrection are not the mechanisms by which God saves, the two levers, as it were, that he pulls to work our redemption. They are, instead, events that are internal to God's own life as Emmanuel.

It is perhaps true that God could have saved us in a different way had he so chosen, but Christmas reminds us that the passion story is a story of God's life as a human being. Remembering the story of Emmanuel at Easter helps us to remember that the way God chose to save was a way with us—not outside of us or over against us or without us, but with us.

Redemption, so the link between Christmas and Easter shows, was worked from the inside. The salvation we celebrate at Easter is a victory from the inside.

The difference this makes for how Easter puts Christians in the world is nothing short of dramatic.

If we are to be in the world as witnesses to God's salvific work in Christ, knowing that God's Easter work is done from inside the human condition puts us in the world as those who are with others as God is with us. Salvation as Christians know it is not merely the declaration to sinners that all is forgiven; it is the living out of forgiveness in the presence of sin—the "with-ness" and work of grace in the midst of regular, sinful human life.

So, too, the victory over death is not only the claim that we shall be raised as Jesus himself was; it is also the assurance in the face of suffering that the life we begin as a baby will not ultimately amount to nothing.

The resurrection is a validation of a life that runs from infancy to death, an emphatic statement by God that he himself—personally, within his own existence as God—is victoriously on the side of a dying humanity.

The resurrection is known in real time as hope in the work of God against that which assails us through dying and death. The unraveling of our plans, the physiological weakness, the isolation even from our most intimate companions, the emotional devastation—in short, all the hints that death is around us and even inside us—do not finally mock us.

Christmas reminds us that Easter does not tell us that our bodily lives will finally be left behind or that the utter seriousness with which we regard a human life is in vain. It says instead that the life history that makes us who we are, broken as it may well be, matters to God enough to save and redeem.

The theologian Martin Kaehler once famously said that the Gospels were passion narratives with long introductions. In a way, he was right.

The Gospels do lead to the passion and the resurrection. But there are profound and important reasons that we have what comes before.

Christmas reminds us that we can never think about the death or the resurrection without the human Jesus, without, that is, understanding their significance in light of God's decision to be with us and for us as a human being. Only then will we begin to see that salvation from sin and death is a statement about the utter and final worth of human life to God.

Notes

Suffering Is Part of Thriving

1. David Bentley Hart, *The Doors of the Sea* (Grand Rapids: Eerdmans, 2011), 104, referencing Dostoevsky's *The Brothers Karamazov*.

Failure as Christ-Shaped Leadership

1. Atul Gawande, *Complications* (New York: Picador, 2002), 62.
2. Charles Bosk, *Forgive and Remember: Managing Medical Failure*, 2nd ed. (Chicago: University of Chicago Press, 2003), xxiii.

Making the Connecions

1. Gregory L. Jones, "Networking, Border Crossing and Staying on Pitch," *Faith and Leadership*, January 3, 2011, https://faithandleadership .com/networking-border-crossing-and-staying-pitch.

Leadership and the Discipline of Silence

1. Søren Kierkegaard, *For Self-Examination; Judge for Yourself*, trans. Howard V. Hong and Edna H. Hong (Princeton: Princeton University Press, 1990), 47-48.

Our Most Significant Experiences Are in Institutions

1. Andy Crouch, *Playing God: Redeeming the Gift of Power* (Downers Grove, IL: InterVarsity Press, 2013), 170.

2. Crouch, *Playing God*, 219.

"Power" in the Christian Sense Is the Concrete Shape of Hope

1. Andy Crouch, *Playing God: Redeeming the Gift of Power* (Downers Grove, IL: InterVarsity Press, 2013), 37.

Leading in the Age of the Image

1. See Andy Crouch, "Visualcy," *Christianity Today*, May 31, 2005, https://www.christianitytoday.com/ct/2005/june/21.62.html.

2. Xiaoqing Gao and Steven Brown, "The Neuroscience of Beauty," *Scientific American*, September 27, 2011, https://www.scientificamerican.com/article/the-neuroscience-of-beauty/.

3. See "Marguerite 'Maggy' Barankitse: Love Made Me an Inventor," *Faith and Leadership*, December 16, 2013, https://faithandleadership.com/marguerite-maggy-barankitse-love-made-me-inventor.

4. George Steiner, *Tolstoy or Dostoevsky* (New Haven: Yale University Press, 1996), 3.

The Church and the Vanishing Neighbor

1. Marc Dunkelman, *The Vanishing Neighbor: The Transformation of American Community* (New York: W. W. Norton, 2014), 97.

2. Dunkelman, *The Vanishing Neighbor*, 111.

3. Dunkelman, *The Vanishing Neighbor*, 111.

Index